SOUTH ASIAN
COOKING

Made Easy for Working Couples

SOUTH ASIAN COOKING

Made Easy for Working Couples

AMTUL HAFEEZ

Rupa & Co

To the people of South Asia

Design, Photographs & Typeset
Art Creations
45 Nehru Apts, Kalkaji
New Delhi 110 019
arrtcreations@gmail.com

Order this book online at www.trafford.com/08-0082
or email orders@trafford.com

Most Trafford titles are also available at major online book retailers.

First Published By Rupa & Co. India 2004

Note for Librarians: A cataloguing record for this book is available from Library
and Archives Canada at www.collectionscanada.ca/amicus/index-e.html

Printed in Victoria, BC, Canada.

ISBN: 978-1-4251-6918-3

*We at Trafford believe that it is the responsibility of us all, as both individuals and corporations, to make choices
that are environmentally and socially sound. You, in turn, are supporting this responsible conduct each time you
purchase a Trafford book, or make use of our publishing services. To find out how you are helping, please visit
www.trafford.com/responsiblepublishing.html*

*Our mission is to efficiently provide the world's finest, most comprehensive book publishing service, enabling
every author to experience success. To find out how to publish your book, your way, and have it available
worldwide, visit us online at www.trafford.com/10510*

 www.trafford.com

North America & international
toll-free: 1 888 232 4444 (USA & Canada)
phone: 250 383 6864 ♦ fax: 250 383 6804 ♦ email: info@trafford.com

The United Kingdom & Europe
phone: +44 (0)1865 722 113 ♦ local rate: 0845 230 9601
facsimile: +44 (0)1865 722 868 ♦ email: info.uk@trafford.com

10 9 8 7 6 5 4 3 2

Contents

INTRODUCTION

I am the oldest member of my family who, at the age of 33, moved permanently 53 years ago from South Asia to North America. Of my three children two were born in India and one in Libya when my husband was working on a UN mission in that country.

All my children have settled in North America. Two are citizens of the United States and one of Canada and they have raised their families in these countries. I have ten grandchildren, of whom four have already reached the marriageable age.

As the head of my growing family in North America it is my responsibility to transfer to my children and grandchildren my cultural heritage of which our traditional South Asian food forms an integral part. My own children, who spent many of their growing years outside my home for educational reasons, have learned from me some of our traditional cuisine and they are following it in their homes. But they continue to ask for my advice as they try to expand, preserve and enrich their knowledge of our cuisine. Again for educational reasons my grandchildren missed out to a much greater extent than my children the opportunity to learn from their mothers even the knowledge of the general approach and background of the cooking of South Asian food. However, from their childhood they are accustomed to eating our traditional foods. While they may enjoy an occasional foray into western and other ethnic foods they are only satisfied when they eat our kind of food which is indeed their staple diet.

My eldest son was first married to a Caucasian American and she took such a great liking to our South Asian food that she went to great lengths to learn from me the cooking of a limited number of our meat and vegetable dishes. Unfortunately they are now divorced but sometime ago their eldest son, Kyle Mumtaz, who had already developed a taste for our food and who now lives and works in Switzerland, made a special visit to learn from me the cooking of some of our food. I gave him some of my pots and pans, especially suited for that kind of cooking. And just a short time ago, my eldest granddaughter, Nuzha, in preparation for her marriage, came to Winnipeg, once again to learn from me the cooking of some of our dishes as her cousin had done before. She actually cooked those dishes directly under my supervision, after she had very carefully written the recipes with full details of the procedures involved. When she returned to California and cooked those dishes again in my daughter's house where she lived, my daughter made a special telephone call to me to say that Nuzha had been eminently successful in bringing out the taste and flavour of those dishes. The fact is that whenever any of my grandchildren make a visit to me, eating the food I cook normally in my house becomes a matter of their prime interest and they not only eat it to the point of gluttony but also carry away bagfuls of the leftovers with them when they go.

When my husband was working for the UN Development Programme in countries of Africa and the Middle East, we almost always had some UN experts from western countries who had lived and worked in India or Pakistan. These experts had eaten our South Asian food there and had never forgotten its delicious taste and flavour and looked forward to my inviting them where they could eat that food again. And even when I specially cooked some western food for them they would leave that alone and go entirely for our food.

When I came to North America in the late forties and began to live in New York city I found that many of the spices and vegetables and some lentils, specially produced in South Asian countries were not available in the local food markets. As I usually went to Pakistan every two years or so I had to bring back with me a sufficient supply of spices and lentils or ask some friend or relative coming to the U.S. from Pakistan to bring them over for me. As a matter of fact some of our lentils, now freely available both in the U.S. and Canadian markets, were so little known in these countries that the U.S. Customs had to pass them as chicken feed when one of my relatives brought them for me from Pakistan!

The style of food in my house has not changed over the entire period of some 53 years I have lived in North America, Africa and the Middle East and all our three children have largely maintained the same style in their homes. The situation now is that in terms of seniority and experience I am perhaps the oldest living custodian among all my new relatives in North America and South Asia who carries the inheritance of the original classical traditional recipes of our South Asian food learned by me from my elders. My daughter and daughters-in-law have learned from me some of the recipes and cooking techniques but because of my long years of experience and the adjustments and adaptation I have made, they still turn to me from time to time for advice and guidance in cooking some of the dishes. Furthermore since I did not go to work outside the home I had the time and the opportunity to experiment intensively so as to adapt and simplify our classical traditional recipes and cooking techniques to the conditions of living in North America and make good use of the appliances and facilities available here.

The fact is that the procedures involved in cooking our food as it is normally done by families in India and Pakistan, is so time-consuming as to occupy more than half a day for a housewife, if she has to do all the culinary work by herself.

For families living in North America the situation is even more difficult. Women who are trained and educated would like to go to work outside and bring the extra money needed to maintain a reasonable standard of living. It also takes them out of the boring monotonous life of staying at home and carrying on with the drudgery of having to cook their traditional style of food day after day soaking their homes with a permanent spicy odour. The alternative which many women have resorted to is to go for pre-cooked western style food, frozen or otherwise, with unknown effects on their health of the chemical preservatives, contained in them, besides the fact that such foreign foods may fill their stomachs but give them no real enjoyment of eating. Such a manner of eating also often creates tensions, between husbands and wives making for unnecessary marital unhappiness.

As I am nearing the end of my life I consider it my duty to my future generations to pass on to them in writing the part of my cultural heritage relating to our South Asian food, adapted to conditions of living and working in North America. I believe such a record would be equally valuable in the South Asian sub-continent where educated women are now going to work outside the home in ever larger numbers. This cultural heritage does not lend itself to be transferred by word of mouth alone. By writing it out I would leave it as a permanent source of guidance and enjoyment for all those who may be interested, for all time to come. This I have attempted to do in the pages which follow.

Amtul Hafeez
Winnipeg, Manitoba
Canada

HISTORY, COMPOSITION & BENEFITS

South Asian food is not any peculiar, exotic or exclusive kind of food as it is generally thought to be by people in some parts of the world. It is in fact a combination of the Indo-European and Caucasian food prepared with a rather extensive range of common spices and herbal ingredients and it is today a product of trials and experimentation extending over many centuries in the past.

The addition of spices in the processing and the cooking of meat or vegetable dishes is determined both by health considerations, as established through centuries of experience, as well as by regional climatic conditions. The seasoning of herbal ingredients such as onions, garlic and other selected spices in the preparation of food is aimed at enhancing the taste and flavour of cooked food, which helps to stimulate the secretion of juices and enzymes in the human digestive system and also provides protection against any inflammatory and other toxic effects arising from the ingestion of food in the stomach.

Some four thousand years ago the great steppland which stretches from Poland to Central Asia was inhabited by semi-nomadic barbarians called the Aryans. As their population grew they started to migrate in bands westward, southward and eastward conquering local populations and forming ruling classes. Like other migrating Aryan bands the food of those who entered the Indian subcontinent mainly consisted of meat and apart from hunting and gathering, they held special ceremonial sacrifices of large animals to provide meat for their food.

However, around 269 BC, when Asoka was the ruler of India, he came under the influence of Buddhism and gave his strong support to the doctrine of Ahimsa (non-injury to man and animals) and placed a limited ban on animal sacrifices regulating the slaughter of animals for food while completely forbidding the killing of certain species, in particular cows. From that period onwards the population of India called Hindus (a name given to them by the Persians derived from the river Indus) moved progressively towards vegetarianism and began to make use of spices in their vegetable preparations initially to make them palatable and tasty and later for health reasons, in the same way as the Aryans who migrated westwards, went out to search for spices in the tropical areas of the world to make their dried meat palatable to them during the winter months.

Over hundreds of years the Hindus developed the art of cooking of vegetables which they eat with bread (baked or fried) made of doughs of different cereals, mainly of wheat. No one today, anywhere in the world, can cook vegetable dishes, called *Subzi*, *Tarkari* or *Bhaji* as perfectly and tastily as it is done today by the Indian families. India's tropical climate also favours the growing of vegetables as well as of spices of a very large variety throughout the year, a variety which is not found anywhere else in the world.

Thus the vegetables and the cereals have provided the Hindus of India with their carbohydrate and vitamin needs while the dairy products and lentils and rice have provided the necessary protein requirements of the diet. Indeed, the vegetables also serve up loads of fibre which delay the absorption of starches and levels out the glucose response. Unfortunately very little information is available in the historical records of the health and social conditions in ancient India when the transformation from a meat eating diet to vegetarianism had taken place. From the scanty remarks contained in the writings of Megasthenes, 305 BC, the Greek envoy of the Bactrian State, and of Fa-Hien, the Chinese traveller who came to India 700 years later one can get a glimpse that the people of India were strong and healthy. In his remarks on social customs Fa-Hien has noted that all respectable people of India were vegetarians, meat eating being confined to the low caste and untouchables. It should be noted, however, that in the coastal regions of India fish and rice was and still remains the staple food of the people. Until the population explosion began in India, around the middle of the nineteenth century leading to some malnutrition among the poor, the majority of the people of India, largely concentrated in the pristine rural areas of the country, were living a healthy life, free from many of the chronic diseases which afflict modern societies today. Indeed, heart disease, diabetes, obesity, cancer of breast, colon and prostate are not so common even today among the people in the South Asian sub-continent.

Then, around the twelfth century A.D. another wave of migration from Central Asia brought a new population to India whose diet consisted mainly of meat. Islam had spread to Central Asia by that time and as the Muslims who came to India, fought wars and settled down, they continued to use meat as their principal diet but also progressively adopted the delicious vegetable food of the local people, the Hindus, as a complementary part of their staple food. However during the sixteenth and seventeenth centuries as the incoming Muslim migrants became the rulers of India, they too, like the Hindus, began to pay greater attention to attaining a higher degree of sophistication in the cooking of meat. During the Mughal rule in India large kitchens were established with liberal budgets, as part of the Emperor's household, in which experiments were conducted in the preparation of meat dishes with a combination of Arabic, Persian, Turkish and Hindu food components and techniques of cooking. These experiments gave birth to what is called the Mughlai, a highly delicious and famous style of cuisine involving the use of meat and though the recipes of such cuisine were at first kept a secret, confined to the nobles and officials of the Emperor's court, they became, over a period of years, the normal style of food of the well-to-do families of the Indian sub-continent.

Thus, the South Asian food of today consists on the one hand of vegetable curries now commonly called *Subzi*, perfected for flavour and taste by the Hindus over a period of centuries and of rice, lentils and dairy products which together provide a complete diet for the Hindu population. The cuisine of the Muslim population, on the other hand, which constitutes nearly one fourth of the population of the sub-continent consists of –

(i)   dishes of pure meat perfected for flavour and taste by the Mughal rulers of India, now called the classical style;

(ii) a mix of meat and vegetable curries, also based on classical methods of cooking;

(iii) pure vegetable dishes in the Hindu style of cooking,

(iv) fish, rice and lentils.

Dairy products, of course, also go along with all this food.

The Muslims have thus adopted for their cuisine what may be called the best of all worlds, and it is this comprehensive range of cuisine, properly called the South Asian food, the methods and techniques of cooking which I learned from my elders and which I have been following ever since I established my own household. The purpose of my writing this book is to pass on to the future generations knowledge I possess of this comprehensive, delicious and valuable cuisine and of the special methods and techniques I have developed from my experience of living for nearly five decades in North America, Africa and the Middle East, so as to make the cooking of South Asian food a much easier and pleasurable experience.

Before proceeding any further I would like to correct an erroneous impression which has come to exist in some parts of the world that South Asian food is "hot" food. This is not at all true. Any food to which chillies or peppers are added becomes "hot" by definition and the larger the added quantities the "hotter" the foods will be. The chillies and peppers when added to food have certain health benefits and they also give it a level of taste. But their amount can be increased or reduced in South Asian food without affecting its overall flavour and taste. For instance, in the cooler regions of India the amount of chillies added to food is much less than in the hotter regions.

Recently an excellent book entitled, *Genetic Nutritioneering,* has come into the market authored by Jeffrey S. Bland, with Sara H. Benum, which has highlighted the results of the research and studies made during the last decade on the important influences of foods upon our health and well-being. We now know that

(a) we are really what we eat — the food we eat is both a source of some of our health problems as well as a means of curing them;

(b) many of the genetic characteristics which can give rise to illness can be modified by the way our genes are treated with dietary factors;

(c) our intestinal tract is the site of nearly two-thirds of the body's defence system. Poor quality of typical diet can stress our genes into expressing their message to the immune system to fight back, which it does by becoming activated and promoting inflammation not only in body's joints but also in any other part of the body.

(d) The food should provide the raw materials needed for carrying out the task of construction and repairs to help our organism in its efforts to maintain what is called Homeostasis ie., to keep everything the same in our body.

(e) It should help to stimulate our appetite and generate the digestive juices, enzymes and hormones needed to break down the food to the point where it can be absorbed in our body.

(f) It should provide protection and also act as a healer against the outbreak of inflammation in any part of our body, which is now known to be the cause of many of our chronic and other diseases.

South Asian food while eminently fulfilling the first and second functions described above also provides valuable help in responding to the third and the fourth functions. It does so through the herbal spices of which the maximum use is made in South Asian food.

From our forefathers down to this day South Asian food has been our staple food. My family and I have been living in North America for nearly 40 years and we have always been eating our standard South Asian food. Now in our middle eighties, we are able to say that we have been living an active and healthy life free from any chronic disease. I am writing this to say that the South Asian food we have been eating has not only helped to keep us alive and active up to our present advanced age, but has also kept us free from any malignancy or other health-wasting problem.

In the January 2002 issue of the *Newsweek,* Janice Horowitz, writing an article under the title "10 Foods That Pack a Wallop" has said, that a clove of garlic in your refrigerator... used correctly (has) the power to prevent all kinds of serious ailments, including heart disease, diabetes and even cancer."

Below is a list of the various spices used in South Asian cooking and their known benefits:

SPICES COMMONLY USED & THEIR KNOWN BENEFITS*

HOT PEPPER (MIRCH) (GREEN OR RED)

Helps to lower response to inflammation-producing substances; useful in controlling nerve damage; rich in Vitamin C.

CILANTRO (HARA DHANIA)

Anti-oxidant; improves fragrance in food. (Leaves) Also called Chinese parsley

CORIANDER (DHANIA) SEEDS

Antioxidant; meat preserver; taste enhancer.

CARDAMOM (ELAICHI) SMALL

Controls nausea, abdominal pain and indigestion; also helps provide relief in bronchitis and respiratory infections.

CUMIN (ZEERA)

Helps in controlling diarrhea, flatulence and stomach disorders.

CARDAMOM (ELAICHI) LARGE

Properties similar to that of cardamom (small).

FENNEL (SAUNF)

Mild expectorant; controls coughing; improves flavour and aroma in food.

GARLIC (LASHAN)

Fights infections; protects against heart disease and stroke; lowers cholesterol; eases blood pressure; nips cancer in the bud with anticarcinogenic properties.

GINGER (ADRAK)

Controls nausea; reduces inflammation associated with arthritis and other related inflammatory disorders.

CLOVE (LAUNG)

Medicinal antiseptic with germicidal properties; appetizer; digestive; breath freshener.

MACE (JOZ)

Relieves bronchial disorders, rheumatism and flatulence, liver and skin complaints.

MINT (PUDINA)

A natural expectorant; reduces asthma, pain in joints; stimulates liver and spleen functions.

* South Asian names of spices are given in brackets.

NUTMEG (JAWETRI)

Helps in teeth and skin protection and cleanup. An additive used as flavouring enhancer.

ONION (PIAAZ)

Anti-inflammatory in arthritis and good for controlling allergic reactions.

BLACK PEPPER (KALI MIRCH)

Anti-spasmodic; helps reduce flatulence and controls diarrhea; also used as a gargle for sore throats.

TURMERIC (HALDI)

Anti-inflammatory; helps control viral hepatitis, sore throat and skin allergies.

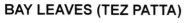

BAY LEAVES (TEZ PATTA)

Controls flatulence; helps in dyspepsia, cough and diabetes mellitus.

SAFFRON (ZAFFRAN)

Taste stimulant, carminative; adds robust aroma to food preparations.

More details of the spices listed above can be found in the monograph - *Selected Medicinal Plants of India* - published by Basic Chemicals, Pharmaceuticals and Cosmetic Export Promotion Council of India. This monograph informs the reader about the therapeutic potential of some Indian Medicinal plants. However, these plants and their products have actually been in use for centuries in the preparation of South Asian cuisine. They have already proved their worth in enhancing the taste and flavour of the prepared food in addition to their known health claims. Throughout my life no one from our part of the world has ever complained of any ill effects of any of these spices. On the other hand I find that their use is gradually expanding in commercial foods in the western world. The September 01 issue of *Readers Digest* contains an article entitled - "The Healing Power of Asian Food" - which describes the well-documented beneficial effects of spices such as ginger and garlic in controlling some chronic diseases. It is my belief that in time to come people throughout the western world would find that a combination of South Asian food (with its well-known anti-obesity benefits of which my husband, myself and my children are an example) along with their usual food would offer them an ideal diet both in terms of nutrition and health.

PREPARATION FOR COOKING

The programme involving some essential preparatory actions I am presenting here has a threefold purpose. First, the actual cooking of the main meals should not be done more than two or a maximum of three times a month. Secondly, the time spent on the cooking of a dish should be cut down by at least a third of the time now spent in the conventional manner of cooking of the same dish. Thirdly, further overall saving of time should be achieved by the elimination of piecemeal purchases of food items with numerous shopping trips.

There are four major components of South Asian food.

1. Meat
2. Spices, Yogurt
3. Vegetables, Lentils, Rice
4. Oils

MEAT

(i) Koftas (meat balls cooked in curry)
(ii) Skewered kebabs (Seekh kebab)
(iii) Spiced patties (Shami kebabs)
(iv) Nahari (now also cooked in homes).

KOFTAS

These are made with ground meat which is readily available in various grades in the food shops. However, the best result cannot be obtained from such ready made ground meat even in its leanest form. For making koftas it is, therefore, preferable to have ground meat made on a custom order basis in a butcher's shop from the leg section cleaned of all its fat layers of fat.

SKEWERED KEBABS (SEEKH KEBAB)

These are also made with ground meat and once again it is best to buy them from a butcher's shop in the same way as koftas.

SPICED MEAT PATTIES (SHAMI KEBABS)

These can be made with ready made extra lean ground meat sold in food shops. Since these patties are fried, the small amount of fat content in the meat helps in the frying process.

NAHARI

This dish is made from meat shanks which are not normally found in the meat counters of the food shops. They should be custom ordered from a butcher's shop along with some marrow bones for which no charge is usually made.

NOTE:

It is necessary to have all meat purchased for koftas, skewered kebabs, spiced meat patties and nahari packed at the butcher's shop, securely in packing paper marked or stamped for later identification and should be placed in the freezer immediately on bringing them home. The bones should also be placed in the freezer though they may be left in the plastic shopping bag.

LAMB OR GOAT MEAT

In South Asian countries the preferred meat for making curries is that of goat. The reason is that goat meat is less fibrous than lamb's and cooks more quickly. However, as the grazing areas in South Asian countries are shrinking rapidly with the growth of human population and goats are more destructive of ground vegetation than lamb, the breeding of lambs and the use of its meat as a substitute for goat's is gaining ground.

Muslims living in North American countries cook their curries almost entirely with lamb meat as goat meat is seldom available in standard food shops. However, even for lamb's meat the food shops usually sell it in the form of chops or whole legs. Fresh lamb is available only in the summer months. In the winter, legs of lamb usually imported from New Zealand are sold in a frozen state, but as this meat carries a certain odour which is not extinguished in the cooking process it is not considered suitable for South Asian curries. Hence the best course to follow is to order a whole lamb from a butcher's shop during the summer and have it cut there by the shop machines roughly into ping pong ball- sized pieces called "Boties" after the removal of layers of fat. The whole lamb to be ordered should be about 25 to 30 pounds in weight. The meat of lambs of higher weight would be more fibrous and would take a longer time in cooking. When the whole lamb's meat, duly cut at the butcher's shop into cooking size pieces for curry, is delivered at home it should be further cleaned of any remaining sticking fat and membranes particularly from meat pieces cut from the areas around the stomach lining. At this stage, the liver, the spleen and the brain should be kept separate from the rest of the meat. Those wishing to cook these parts should cut them into cookable pieces at home; otherwise they may be left at the butcher's shop to be disposed of there.

The cleaned up pieces of the entire meat of the whole lamb are now ready for packing into freezer bags. For convenience it is best to do the packing into medium-size zippered freezing bags in such a manner that each bag contains as much as possible a mixture of meat from different parts. Normally, after the removal of fat, the membranes and other unwanted parts of a whole lamb of 25 to 30 pounds in weight would yield a net cooking weight of about 18 to 22 pounds. Even so it would be far cheaper than buying lamb's meat in smaller amounts from food or butcher shops.

As soon as the meat has been packed at home in freezer bags it should be transferred to the freezer. My experience has shown that fresh meat kept in the freezer for some weeks, when defrosted, cooks better than fresh meat.

POULTRY

Poultry is normally available in food shops in whole or cut up in parts, as well as specialized parts such as legs, breast or wings. All these, however, are sold with the skin attached. South Asians generally cook the poultry either in curried form or with rice, though they have now begun to fry, bake and barbeque the chicken parts as well turned into ground form. In all cases, however, the skin should preferably be removed along with any fat and superfluous membranes. For currying purposes all parts of poultry should be cooked together and therefore whole chickens should be purchased, cut up in parts. For freezing purposes several chickens should be bought at a time and after taking off the skin, fat and superfluous membranes each chicken should be packed separately in freezer bags and transferred to the freezer.

SPICES, YOGURT

Under my suggested programme when the cooking of any dish is undertaken, it should be done in such quantities as to provide for several meals, for immediate use as well as for storage. Hence most of the dry spices listed in this chapter should be bought in adequate quantities to cover the cooking of at least two or three different dishes in bulk quantities whether it is done all at one time or at different times. I usually cook one bulk dish at a time so that I can give it my full attention and make sure that it is perfectly done and no step is missed.

Again, to save time, both the fresh, green and the dry spices should be handled as follows:

FRESH & GREEN SPICES
(Onions, Ginger, Garlic and Cilantro)

The onions should be bought in bags of 10 or 20 pounds; ginger and garlic in a minimum of two pounds each and cilantro in two or four bunches.

The onions should be peeled, cut and chopped in the quantity required at the time of cooking according to the recipe of the particular dish involved.

When buying ginger it is a good practice to test the large root pieces by breaking them slightly in a corner to be sure that they are not too fibrous. On bringing it home, the ginger should be washed thoroughly and then peeled to a smooth surface. Thereafter each large piece should be placed on a hard board and cut into fine lengths and then spread on a flat steel or aluminum pan, which should be placed in the stove oven under the oven light only. The heat generated by the light will remove the surface moisture of the finely cut pieces and this ginger when soaked later in the water will return largely to its fresh condition. The dried ginger can be stored in a jar with a tight lid in the kitchen cabinet to be available for use in cooking when required. It would remain good for use for several months and repeated action for preparing the ginger can be avoided.

As for the garlic it is preferable to use it along with ginger, in cooking South Asian dishes. Therefore, as a first step the cloves should be separated from the garlic bulb and the covering of each clove removed to bring out the smooth kernel. Side by side an equal amount of ginger should be cleaned, peeled and cut into small pieces. Then after putting a small amount of olive oil in the blender both the garlic cloves and the ginger should be ground together to a paste-like condition. This paste should be stored, again with a small amount of olive oil added to it, in a jar with a tight lid and kept in the refrigerator. The combined paste of garlic and ginger would then be ready for use as and when the two spices are needed together. This is again a part of the preparatory work which would take a lot of burden off one's hands at the time the cooking work is in process.

The cilantro is used in two ways — to cook particular dishes as well as in its fresh green form. For cooking purposes, after the cilantro has been thoroughly washed and drained it should be chopped bunchwise along with its stems over a hard board with a serrated knife and then kept ready to be added to the cooking pot as required. For use in its fresh form the leaves should be picked off the stems and kept ready to be eaten in their green form as a flavouring agent, along with certain meat dishes, as will be described in the concerned recipes .

DRY SPICES

The use of any particular dry spice or a set of them is determined by the kind of dish which is to be prepared. Some of the spices can, however, be combined in advance and kept ready for use as the occasion arises — again as a measure of reducing the burden of work and saving of time. Two combinations of dry spices are generally prepared for this purpose. One is called Garam Masala and the other Chat Masala.

GARAM MASALA

This is made up of the following spices:
- Cloves
- Black Pepper
- Cardamom (large — peeled)
- Cumin Seeds, Zeera

Grind equal amounts of these spices, e.g., two tablespoons of each. After these four ingredients have been dry ground in a blender, the powdered mixture should be kept in a jar with a tight lid and kept along with other dry spices in the kitchen cabinet for use as and when needed.

CHAT MASALA

The recipes of this masala are legion and it can be bought ready made in Asian spice shops. This masala is intended to be a taste enhancer whether it is used in the cooking of dishes particularly of pure vegetables or directly by sprinkling over a fruit salad or slightly dipping in it any piece of fruit while eating. This way of using the masala makes the eating of citrus fruits particularly delicious. It is actually a South Asian MSG (Monosodium Glutamate) which is commonly used in Chinese and Japanese cuisine to enhance the taste of their dishes. This masala is made with a combination of dry spices and there are numerous ways in which the various spices are combined to produce a variety of tastes. The ground red pepper and cumin seeds are of course, common to all Chat masalas but the real difference is made by other kinds of salts which are used. For instance, to the common salt there are added other special salts produced in South Asian countries under the names of Nowsader, Kala Namak and Tatri (now also available in spice shops in Europe and North America) which produce a special piquant kind of taste. Hence when buying commercially available masalas one should see whether these contain such special salts. Such masala can, of course, also be made at home by a combination of the desired spices with the special salts mentioned above in discreet quantities and adjusting the amount of red pepper. This masala, whether bought commercially or made at home should be kept handy for use directly in fruit salads or as a taste enhancer in cooking vegetable dishes.

YOGURT

Yogurt is an essential ingredient in South Asian cuisine. Apart from its nutritional value it works as a souring agent and helps to mix the different spices, modifies their pungent character and adds to the flavour of gravy in the curries.

Natural yogurt is normally sold in all food shops where milk is sold. The labels on the yogurt containers, however, do not always indicate the type of culture used for incubation which makes a difference in the taste, flavour and texture of the product. The process of making yogurt at home is, however, quite simple and easy and one can be sure of its quality and freshness. I have always made my own yogurt with two litres of milk at a time, which I use for all my cooking needs and also for eating it directly as a salad supplement with certain foods. The method I use for making yogurt is as follows:

1. Pour into a double boiler 2 litres of milk (either homogenized, raw, 2% or skimmed). Add to cold milk ½ cup of non-fat milk powder. This is optional though it adds to the firmness of yogurt.

2. Heat milk to boiling point.

3. Cool milk to room temperature.

4. Add to milk one tablespoonful of yogurt culture. Mix well with a beater. (How to obtain yogurt culture is explained later.)

5. Pour the incubated milk into medium size glass jars rinsed with boiling water. Cover the jars with stretch and seal.

6. Place the jars on a 12" pizza plate and transfer them into the oven under the oven light only i.e. without opening the oven.

The firming up of the incubated milk under the heat of the oven light usually takes 3 to 5 hours. This can be checked by taking out a jar from the oven and shaking it lightly to see if the surface was firmed up. Then take the glass jars out of the oven while still on the tray and leave them on the kitchen counter for one or two hours to cool down. The jars may then be transferred into the refrigerator and the yogurt will be further firmed up and be ready for use in some 12 hours or so.

Before using yogurt save some four tablespoonfuls in a small jar previously rinsed in boiling water. This yogurt will serve as a culture to prepare the next batch of yogurt.

It is advisable to renew the yogurt culture monthly to prevent the progressive contamination from air, utensils, containers, hands, clothes etc., and to eliminate defects due to faulty techniques and aging of yogurt culture.

Good quality yogurt culture can be bought from health food stores which sell vitamins of natural source.

VEGETABLES, LENTILS, RICE

VEGETABLES

In South Asian cuisine the following vegetables may be cooked with meat as well as without meat. Those vegetables which are cooked with meat are called "Salans" or curries and those which are cooked without meat are called "Subzi" or "Tarkari". (The meat which is cooked without vegetables is called "Sada Salan or Quorma".)

BEET (CHOQANDER)

For this vegetable both the roots as well as the leaves are used in cooking. Beets are usually sold in bunches of four or five units with their leaves attached and that is the way they should be bought, because it is the combination of roots and leaves which enhances the taste of the dish. When buying the beets it should be noted, however, that the leaves have a fresh look and are not excessively crumpled or damaged. In preparing them for cooking, the leaves should be separated from the roots and washed thoroughly and thereafter cleaned of all damaged parts. The beet roots should also be washed and their outer skin peeled away. They should then be sliced into strips about one inch long and a sixth of an inch in width. As for the leaves, hold them in small bunches in hand and placing them on a hard cutting board, cut them along with the stems about an inch and a half apart. The strips of the roots and the leaves so cut should then be mixed together and kept ready for transfer into the cooking pot at the time indicated in the recipe for this dish.

BITTER MELON OR BITTER GOURD (KARELA)

Two varieties of this vegetable are normally sold in the food shops. One is a Chinese variety which is yellowish, of a smooth surface, and about 9 inches long. The other is imported from India or Fiji and is green in colour, about 6 to 8 inches long and has a ribbed surface. The latter variety provides a better flavour and taste than the former one in South Asian cooking. This vegetable is cooked both with meat and without meat. For cooking in either case the ribs should be peeled off with a peeler and slicing each unit across in two parts, it should be emptied of its contents which also include the seeds. These seeds should be taken out of their soft shells and used as indicated in the recipe. For cooking with meat the shells should be left intact to be filled with ground meat as indicated in the recipe. For making "Subzi" the shells should be sliced in small pieces roughly about half a square inch. They will then be ready for cooking as a "Subzi" by themselves or with "Channa" Dal (Lentil).

CARROTS (GAJAR)

These are good for making a delicious dessert called Gajar ka Halwa of which a recipe is given.

CAULIFLOWER (GOBI)

Both the flowers and the stems of this vegetable are used in South Asian cooking. Cauliflowers should be bought with their leaves attached and it should be noted that they look fresh and green and the flowers are clean white without any smudges upon them. Cauliflowers are cooked both with meat pieces as well as with ground meat. The outer green leaves are to be discarded. The flowers kept intact should be separated in individual pieces and the stem smoothed with a peeler should be sliced in about half inch small pieces and they should be used together or separately according to the relevant recipe. Only the flowers are normally used with ground meat and so is the case in cooking them as a "Subzi" only.

EGG PLANT (BAIGAN)

Three different varieties of this vegetable are usually sold in the food shops — a bulbous large round one, a sleek long one, of about 6 to 9 inches and a small round one of about the size of a golf ball. The latter two varieties are suitable for South Asian cooking with meat or just as a vegetable dish. For cooking either way, they should be cut in small pieces and the stems should be removed and discarded, though it is believed that the stems contain a concentration of nutrients and in a cooked dish their juice can be chewed off. In vegetable dishes the egg plant is best cooked with small pieces of potatoes which enhances their taste and flavour.

OKRA (BHINDI)

These are cooked with meat as a curry or as a pure vegetable dish. When buying them make sure that they are green and fresh looking and are of medium thickness. If they are too thick the shells become fibrous and dry and the seeds become hard. As a result they lose much of their flavour and taste. In preparing them for cooking, the top stems should be peeled off roundly and the thread-like endings should be nipped without making any large openings at either end. In making curry, the bhindis are cooked in whole form whereas for making "Subzi" they should be cut in half inch pieces. When the bhindis are cooked as a Salan (curry), they should be thoroughly dipped in soft yogurt and lemon juice in a bowl for a few minutes before being transferred to the cooking pot.

PEAS (MATAR)

Peas are best cooked in curry with meat or as a vegetable dish with potatoes when they are available in their pods in the growing season. The seeds have their best flavour and taste at that time. When buying them it should be noted that the pods look green and fresh and have not become overripe that is when the pods turn brownish. Only the seeds of the peas are used in cooking. The shells are discarded. Frozen peas could also be cooked in the same way.

POTATOES (ALOO)

These are cooked, either with meat pieces or with ground meat. They are also used for making a 'Subzi' alone or with peas. Choose the smooth pink medium size variety with a minimum number of eyes on the surface. For cooking purposes the skin should be peeled off and the eyes cleaned out. In the meat curry they should be cut in two halves or in four parts if they are above the medium size. For making 'Subzi' they should be sliced in small pieces.

SQUASH LONG (DRAZ GHIA)

Choose those of medium length and circumference making sure they are hard when pressed. Also they should have a fresh green look. They are used both with meat for making a curry as well as for a vegetable dish. The thick skin of the squash should be removed with a peeler to bring out the inside white surface. They should then be cut lengthwise and the two halves of the squash should then be sliced in slanting form (called Lauzat), in pieces about two inches long and an inch wide, which would then be ready for transfer to the cooking pot at the appropriate time as indicated in the recipe.

SQUASH ROUND (MITHA GHIA)

This is sold in food shops in whole or cut into parts. The North American squash is somewhat different in taste and flavour than that produced in South Asian countries where it is used both for cooking the curry as well as for making a vegetable dish. South Asians in North America use this squash almost entirely for the vegetable dish. For this purpose it is preferable to buy it in cut parts and it should be noted that it has a fresh look with a nice yellow colour and is free from any internal deterioration. This squash has a very thick skin which cannot be removed by a peeler and has to be cut out with a sharp knife carefully to avoid injury. After the skin has been removed the squash should be cut in cubes of about an inch and a half for cooking as a vegetable dish.

TOMATO (TAMATAR)

These are used in some South Asian dishes as a souring agent and as a substitute for dried raw mango slices called "Khatai" (normally not available in any North American food shops). The tomatoes should be cut in slices and transferred into the cooking pot at the appropriate time as indicated in the related recipes.

TURNIPS (SHULJUM)

Select turnips which are fresh looking, of medium size and hard when pressed. Wash thoroughly and peel off the outer skin and cut off the hard leaf base. Now, round off each peeled turnip into the shape of a small ball and cut the peelings so obtained into small pieces. These latter peelings should be transferred into the cooking pot with the rounded turnips when making a turnip salan as they will help to enhance the taste of the gravy and also give it a degree of thickness.

ZUCCHINI (TORAI)

This is not exactly the "Torai" grown in South Asian countries but it has its resemblance and also a part of its taste and flavour. It is at best a tolerable substitute. Zucchini can be cooked with meat as well as for a pure vegetable dish. In either case peel only half of its skin, all around and then cut it into thin round slices for cooking.

LENTILS (DALS)

The lentils commonly used in South Asian cooking are: Masoor (Red & Black), Moong, Arhar, Channa and

Urad. Of these only the Channa Dal is cooked both by itself and with meat or vegetables. Moong can be cooked with squash, raw papaya, bitter melon, cauliflower and turnips. All other lentils are cooked by themselves.

Except for Masoor Dal, which should be washed before cooking, all other lentils must be soaked in semi-hot water for about two hours prior to cooking.

Since lentils form a part of the staple diet of the Hindu population of India, and a supplementary part of the cuisine of the Muslims, their quality has been improved a great deal and the hot and humid climate of the sub-continent in which the lentils are grown also gives them a better flavour and taste. Therefore lentils should preferably be bought from South Asian food shops which usually import their supplies from India or Pakistan.

RICE (CHAWAL)

The Basmati Rice is the preferred quality of rice for South Asian cooking. It is a thin long rice and has a special flavour and fragrance of its own. India and Pakistan are the main sources of supply of Basmati rice where the climate favours the growing of this quality of rice. The best quality Basmati rice is grown in the province of Punjab in Pakistan, where its blooms spread their subtle fragrance far and wide in the countryside. The Arab countries and Iran generally buy up the entire production of Basmati rice grown in Pakistan but some rice does find its way to the North American market. Basmati rice grown in India, particularly in the Dehra Dun area is also of a comparable quality and is sold in South Asian food shops under a number of brand names.

Since the rice cooked in various forms in South Asian cuisine makes a very tasty and refined dish one should always go for the best quality of Basmati rice, trying out the various brand names before settling down to the best one.

The only preparatory work for cooking of rice is to see that it is free of any extraneous materials, such as small stones or fibres which should be picked out and it should then be thoroughly washed before cooking.

OILS (TEL)

Oil or fat is an essential part in the cooking of South Asian food just as it is an indispensable component of a balanced diet. From the earliest date of Aryan settlement in the Indian sub-continent and the domestication of buffaloes and cows, the fat derived from their milk called ghee has been used in the cooking of food. This ghee has a self-preserving quality and when kept well covered in a container it will remain free of rancidity for a long time.

Ghee has continued to be used from ancient times right up to this day for the cooking of all South Asian food. But as the price of ghee has been continually rising and with growing consciousness of possible health risk from the use of animal fat, vegetable oils derived from mustard, sesame, cotton seeds, peanuts and canola have begun to be used as a substitute wholly or partially. The fact remains, however, that ghee provides the best flavour and taste in South Asian food and any substitutes for it can only serve as a second best alternative.

In the house of my parents, as far as my memory goes, ghee was always used for cooking food in our house. And when I established my own house after my marriage I continued the same practice, always trying to find, wherever possible, the ghee prepared in its pure form. There is a well-known saying in India "Ghee Banai Salana — Bari Bahoo ka Naam." (Ghee makes the delicious curry but credit for it is taken away by the senior daughter-in-law cooking in the house.)

However, when I moved to North America some 50 years ago and settled in New York I made enquiries and found that ghee was not produced anywhere in the U.S. I then bought the butter sold in slab form in the food shops and tried to extract ghee from it but found that the process by which the butter was made in North America was such that it did not lend itself to produce ghee. I then consulted some South Asians living in New York and was told that they had been using the Crisco shortening for cooking their food. I then started cooking my food with Crisco and though it did not produce anything like the taste and flavour of food cooked with ghee, I had no alternative but to accept it reluctantly. As time passed the old taste of ghee in our food was forgotten and thanks to our methods and technique of cooking I managed to retain some of our customary taste of food by using Crisco.

After living in New York for nearly ten years I moved to the Middle East and Africa and in countries where Crisco was not available. I used olive oil for our cooking though it proved to be even less suitable than Crisco.

I have now been living in Canada for some 26 years. With Crisco available here I used it for sometime but when Canola vegetable oil came into the market and I tried it for our cooking I found that it came closer in taste and flavour to ghee than any of the other substitutes I had used. For some 20 years or so the Canola oil has therefore been my cooking medium and I use it both for cooking our curries as well as for frying purposes.

EQUIPPING THE KITCHEN

Finally, a well-equipped kitchen containing all the essential pots and pans of the right size and quality and the necessary tools and appliances is a *sine qua non* to achieving the maximum economy of time and ease of operation in cooking food. An over-equipped kitchen is just as bad as one which is under-equipped. A cluttered kitchen may present a rich nice look but it is an invitation to confusion. And a want of the necessary appliances and tools can lead both to a waste of time and possible accidents and injury.

To start with, pots and pans are naturally the most important utensils for a kitchen. This seems to be a simple matter but the large variety of them on display in kitchen stores can easily lead to expensive mistakes in the selection of the right ones needed for different kinds of cooking. For South Asian cooking the most suitable pots are those which have a thick and heavy bottom of the order of "three ply". These permit a steady seasoning of spices and herbs to take place without burning and their subsequent maturation in the final stages of cooking to bring out their full taste and flavour.

On the next page is a list of essential equipment, appliances and tools which are required to furnish the kitchen so as to obtain optimum operational efficiency and convenience. It should be emphasized that when buying any of these kitchen items quality should never be sacrificed for cheapness. It must be realised that food is the most enjoyable and sustaining aspect of our life and the better it is cooked by the use of good quality equipment and tools, the greater its enjoyment and health benefits. The list given below includes only the essential items required for the cooking of South Asian food and not for eating or other decorative purposes. Other items may, of course, be added as the need may arise.

Items	Quantity	Description/Specification
Pots	5	of 8, 6, 4, 2, & 1 Quarts each.
Pans	5	2 of cast iron, one large and one medium and
Pans		3 others of small sizes, thick bottom.
Bowls	5	Large, medium and smaller sizes
Colander	2	Metal, 1 large and 1 of medium size
Drainer Bowls	3	Medium to small sizes
Spoons (cooking)	4	3 plastic & 1 wooden long handled
Fork (serving)	1	Steel bladed, long handled
Spatula	1	Steel bladed, long handled
Spatula	1	Plastic
Spoons (ladle)	1	Steel bladed, long handled
Skimmer	1	Steel bladed, long handled
Beater	1	Strong plastic or steel
Knives	5	1 Long serrated
Knives		1 Long straight edge
Knives		1 Medium half serrated
Knives		1 Paring medium
Knives		1 Paring, small
Cutting Boards	1	Large, Plastic or wood
Cutting Boards	1	Medium, Plastic or wood
Peeler	1	Steel bladed, strong
Masher	1	Plastic or Steel
Egg Holders	4	Stainless steel
Sifter	1	Steel or plastic
Strainer	1	Steel
Oven Mitts	1	Pair

ELECTRIC APPLIANCES

Microwave Oven	1	Medium size
Food Processor	1	Medium size
Blender	1	Medium size
Can Opener	1	
Carving Knife	1	
Mixer	1	

TOOLS

Scissors	2	1 Large and 1 small.
Plier	1	Medium size
Hammer	1	Small
Nut cracker	1	

CLASSIFICATION &

TECHNIQUES OF COOKING

We can now begin to lay out the easiest possible way by which the cooking of South Asian food can be undertaken.

In general, South Asian cuisine can be classified as follows:

SALANS (CURRIES)

Salan is the broad name for all spiced dishes made with meat pieces or ground meat with or without vegetables. They form the basic cuisine of South Asian food and are an integral part of some 70 per cent of all meals. Eaten with whole wheat bread, fried or baked, supplemented with green salads, they provide together our protein, carbohydrate and vitamin needs while conferring protective and healing benefits on our health. They are a simple and satisfying form of food evolved over centuries of experience. And they have now been made more easy to cook both with economy of time and frequency of work, with over several decades of trials and experiments I have made, living both in South Asian and North American countries.

These Salans may be cooked with vegetables or without vegetables as follows:

WITH VEGETABLES

*Aloo ka Salan (curry with potatoes)
Bhindi ka Salan (curry with okra)
Ghia ka Salan (curry with long squash)
Shuljum ka Salan (curry with turnips) etc.

WITHOUT VEGETABLES

Sada Salan (curry with meat pieces only)
Korma (a Mughal form of curry with meat pieces)

---

* Peas can also be added with this Salan

Nahari (a special curry of shank pieces with bone marrow)
Murghi ka Salan (curry with chicken pieces)

SALANS MADE WITHOUT GRAVY (SHURWA)

Aloo Keema ka Salan (potatoes with ground meat)
Baigan ka Salan (egg plant with meat pieces or ground meat)
Gobi ka Salan (cauliflower with meat pieces or ground meat)
Karela ka Salan (bitter melon with ground meat)

KEBABS

Shami kebab (spiced ground meat patties, fried)
Seekh kebab (spiced ground meat skewered, barbequed)

SUBZIS (VEGETABLE DISHES)

These dishes are generally made with the following vegetables:

Aloo	Potatoes
Ghia	Squash — long & round
Bhindi	Okra
Shuljum	Turnip
Torai	Zucchini
Sags	Spinach - Rapini
Tamatar	Tomatoes

RICE

The rice can be cooked with meat or without meat.

WITH MEAT

Biryani simple
Biryani Mughlai

WITHOUT MEAT

Khuska (Plain Rice)
Khichri (Rice with lentils)
Qubuli (Rice with split lentil - channa dal)

Matar Pulao (Rice with peas)

Tahari (Rice with potatoes)

Sweet Rice (in various forms)

COOKING TECHNIQUES

For cooking all the Salans I have formulated a **Composite Masala** which can be put together quickly, ready to be added to the cooking pot at the appropriate time as will be seen in the recipe. This **Composite Masala** saves at least 40 per cent of the time which would otherwise be spent if the various ingredients had to be made up individually at the time the cooking is in process, which is normally done in most South Asian households. Considering that some 70 per cent of the daily South Asian meals are made up of Salans a considerable saving of time is achieved by making use of the **Composite Masala** made up of the following standard ingredients and kept ready in a bowl at the time of cooking.

COMPOSITE MASALA

(The quantities shown are based on cooking one pound of meat with or without vegetables)

Ingredients/Quantities

Ginger and Garlic:

2 tbsp. The mixture of these (Combined — made into paste) two items stands ready in prepared form of paste.

Coriander (Ground):

3 tbsp. Commercially available.

Red Pepper (Ground):

1 tbsp. Commercially available. The quantity may be reduced according to acceptability.

Yogurt:

4 tbsp. Homemade should be preferred over that commercially available.

Salt:

1 tsp. or according to taste.

Turmeric*:

¼ tsp.

DEEP SEASONING (BHOONNA)

This is a special process in South Asian cooking and since there is really no equivalent word in the English language for the native word "Bhoonna", I have used **Deep Seasoning** as the closest expression I could find to describe the process.

The cooking of Salans starts at first with the frying of chopped onions in oil. The **Composite Masala** I have described earlier is then added to the fried onions and mixed thoroughly. (Hold at this time a fine mesh screen above the pot to prevent back-spattering.) Now, keep stirring adding some water until the masala becomes lumpy. The meat is now transferred into the pot and mixed thoroughly with the spices. The main process of "Bhoonna" now starts with the stirring of the meat in the pot round and round with sprinklings of water until the meat has released its moisture and assumed a clean pinkish brown look. At this stage the oil will get separated from the meat and collect around its edges. The penetration of spices in the meat has now taken place.

It should be noted that the process of "Bhoonna" is a key process in the cooking of Salans (curries) in South Asian cooking. It needs very careful attention and eye judgement to see what is actually happening in the pot and regulate the heat from time to time to make sure that the cooking of meat in the **Composite Masala** is taking place in the desired manner. South Asian people among themselves give credit to some women by saying that they possess what is called "a taste in their hands". What it means in actual practice is that some women apply the process of "Bhoonna" in a more perfectionist manner than the others and that makes all the difference. For the beginners it may take some three or four times of practice to master the art of

* not to be used in Salans cooked without vegetables

"Bhoonna" but once the eye judgement is established, it becomes a routine process.

GRAVY (SHURWA & LUAB)

In Salans where gravy (Shurwa) is intended to be obtained a sufficient quantity of water is added after the process of "Bhoonna" is completed so as to stand about an inch or so above the meat, and on full heat with the pot covered, it is checked from time to time until the required amount of gravy is left on the top. In certain Salans it is desirable to have an inch or more of gravy (Shurwa) left floating on the top under a golden layer of oil called "Tar". In other Salans where "Shurwa" is not desired the liquid may be allowed to evaporate to a minimum leaving the top with its golden oil   called "Luab".

MATURATION (DUM)

When the cooking of Salan is completed as described above, what remains to be done is to put it through a process of maturation called "Dum". The idea is to bring out to the full extent the flavour and taste of the dish which is being produced. In South Asian countries this final stage of cooking of Salans was achieved in the past by placing the pot, covered with its lid, over the hot ashes of the fuel, whether of charcoal or other local fuel, and to let the maturation (Dum) of the Salan take place as the ashes gradually cool down. South Asians living in North America cook their Salans on electric or gas stoves. I cook my food on the electric stove and have found a way to produce "Dum" by first raising the burner to full red heat and then immediately closing it. As the heat generated by the burner slows down to final extinction, "Dum" is successfully achieved. The same action can be taken on gas stoves.

BAGHAR

This is another special process in South Asian cooking where in certain dishes a charge of a suitable spice fried in oil is given in certain dishes in the final stage of cooking. See related recipes.

MEAT PREPARATION

When the meat is purchased from a food shop or a butcher some blood, fat and some veins and membranes always stick to it. These have the effect of giving the meat a certain odious smell which is not totally extinguished in the cooking process and detracts to some extent from the refined flavour and taste of the meat dish, which is intended to be achieved in South Asian cooking.

This problem is solved by boiling the meat with some bay leaves and cloves before putting it through the cooking process. The boiling has the effect of melting the sticking fat and softening or removing the superficial veins and membranes and producing the natural smell of meat. After the meat has been put through the boiling process it should then be emptied from the pot into the kitchen sink, previously thoroughly rinsed and disinfected. Each piece of meat should then be inspected and further cleaned as necessary under running water and then transferred into a colander to drain out any water. Meat is then ready to be transferred to the cooking pot in a very clean condition.

PRESERVATION & STORAGE

I have in my freezer a sufficient supply of main meals as well as vegetable side dishes to last us for some three months or so even if I did not do any cooking at all during that period.

Some people have a pre-conceived notion, and South Asians in particular, that frozen food loses some of its nutritional value as well as its natural taste and flavour. They have of course, been right in thinking in that manner, as it is true that in the past freezing appliances had not been developed to the stage where very low temperatures could be maintained consistently to 'lock up' any prepared food in the same chemical state in which it was frozen. The present day freezing appliances have overcome this problem and during the last few years, the food shops have been constantly expanding the sale of cooked frozen food, both in cabinets and open lane freezers, and chain stores such as M & M are doing a roaring business in selling cooked food of all kinds in a frozen state.

It is extremely important, however that any cooked food intended for freezing should be handled in accordance with the established scientific rules to safeguard against any bacterial intrusion and should be defrosted and warmed up before eating in such a manner as not to lose its original taste, flavour and aroma. In South Asian food, the subtle aroma is so critically important that any lapse in following the requisite techniques, the entire process can easily end up in a tasteless dish. It should be remembered that freezing, when properly done, will retain the taste and flavour; it cannot improve quality.

There are, of course, some limits on the storage times of different kinds of foods. The tests which have been made by companies engaged in the freezing technology have helped to determine the optimum duration of storage times of various kinds of foods as follows:

SUGGESTED STORAGE TIMES FRESH MEATS

	Months
Ground and Stew Meats	3 — 4
Lamb and mutton	6 —12

Cooked Meats	
Cooked meat and meat dishes	2 — 3
Gravy and meat broth	2 — 3

	Months
Fresh Poultry	
Chicken and Turkey	12
Chicken pieces	9

Cooked Poultry	
Cooked Poultry Dishes	4 — 6
Fried Chicken	4

Cooked Fish	
Shell Fish	Up to 4
Lean Fish	6 — 8

Shrimp	3

As I have said earlier there are some strict rules for freezing cooked food which must be scrupulously observed. Based upon my experience of nearly 20 years I am setting out these rules below:

GENERAL FREEZING RULES

1. Keep work area thoroughly clean and disinfected from time to time.

2. Choose correct packaging material such as that approved by *Good Housekeeping*, *Betty Crocker*, etc. Both rigid containers and plastic wrappers (for vegetables) can be used. Make sure that they are especially designed for freezing.

3. Fill containers properly. When packing liquid or semi-liquid food in containers, leave about an inch at the top for expansion during freezing.

4. Freeze correct quantities at a time. There is an established maximum for food your freezer is designed to freeze at one time — approximately 3 lbs. per cubic feet of freezer capacity in normal position.

5. Continuously rotate frozen foods to the top of the freezer so that the longest frozen food is used first.

FREEZING OF COOKED FOOD

In practical terms the following procedure should be strictly followed in the freezing of cooked food:

1. Allow the food in the pot in which the food has been cooked to cool down.

2. Bring the pot to the kitchen table and putting it on a heat resistant place tilt the pot slightly forward by inserting a sink stopper at the bottom of the pot.

3. In the case of Salans (curries) with gravy (Shurwa) take out with a spoon in a deep bowl about 1/3 of the golden liquid (Tar) floating on the top of gravy in the pot and put it aside for use as explained under step 5 below.

4. Now take out the food from the pot with a long handled spoon and fill into plastic containers (which have been previously washed in a dishwasher) the amount of food enough to provide a liberal meal serving for two persons or more according to the requirements.

5. When all the food from the pot has been transferred into the plastic containers, the golden liquid previously taken out in a bowl (step 3) should be taken out in small portions with a spoon and used to top up the gravy into those plastic containers which may appear to be filled somewhat less than the others with the golden liquid (Tar). The idea is that when the container is defrosted and the Salan is warmed up for eating it should have the look of a freshly cooked Salan.

6. Now tear up small pieces of a masking tape, stick them firmly on the covers of the plastic containers and write upon them with a wide tipped pen the name of the food which has been packed.

7. Leave the plastic containers lined up on the kitchen dining table to allow the food to cool down further and then fix the covers on the containers making sure they are tightly closed.

8. Some three to four hours thereafter transfer all the containers into the refrigerator and leave them there for some 12 to 14 hours, preferably overnight.

9. Then take all the containers to the freezer (preferably in a large serving tray to avoid any spilling from the containers) and place them one on top of the other along one of the walls of the freezer making sure they are well supported and will not topple over. (This will not be a problem once the food in the containers has frozen.)

10. The freezer should be so packed with every new addition of food that it should be possible to take out one or more containers at any time without

upsetting all other containers stored and that the longest frozen food can be taken out first for use.

11. As more additions of food are made in the freezer, the packing of food in it should be so arranged that when frozen food is withdrawn a different menu should come to hand.

(For quick freezing large amounts of food turn the control knob of the freezer to No.7 two hours before loading. Then return to the normal temperature No. 4 after freezing is completed).

DEFROSTING & WARMING OF FOOD BEFORE EATING

Before setting out the procedure for defrosting and warming of frozen food I should say at the outset that the use of microwave oven is not suitable for that purpose. The meat pieces in the food so defrosted would turn blackish and dry and some of the flavour and aroma of the dish would also be lost. Hence the microwave oven, which may seem to be a quick way of moving the food from the freezer to the dining table, should not be used in defrosting and warming of South Asian food.

The proper steps to be followed for defrosting and warming of South Asian food before eating are set out below:

1. Take out from the freezer in the morning the container of food intended to be eaten that day and leave it in a corner of the kitchen counter with its lid closed.

2. By late afternoon the food will be thawed sufficiently in the carton to be emptied easily into a pot.

3. One hour or so before meal time open one of the burners of the stove to its maximum and then shut it off immediately.

4. Leave the pot on that burner and its diminishing heat will bring about a further slow thawing of the food.

5. Some 20 minutes or so before sitting down for eating reopen the burner to about one-third of its maximum capacity and allow the food warming to take place to the point when small bubbles begin to appear on the surface of the food in the pot and then leave burner at its lowest level until you are ready to eat.

This method of defrosting and warming should be carefully and scrupulously followed and it will be seen that the food so treated, when eaten, will have about the same taste, flavour and aroma as if it had been cooked the same day.

LONG-TERM USE OF FROZEN FOOD

One of my objectives in writing this book is to make the cooking of South Asian food for a working couple and others less onerous, less time consuming and eliminating to a great extent the proverbial drudgery of the kitchen. It means then that not only should the time spent in the cooking of the food be cut down drastically without sacrificing its quality and regular availability on the dining table, but also the frequency with which the cooking is to be undertaken.

I have said earlier that the cooking of a single meat and vegetable dish called 'Salan' in the normal conventional manner in which it is done at present in the large majority of South Asian houses can well occupy the better part of a day for a householder. The methods and techniques I have developed will now make it possible to produce the same dish in about half that time. Furthermore, the frequency of cooking of the same kind of dish will now be cut down from the present three to four times a week to about once in two weeks and even as far as once in a month. These results can be achieved by cooking the individual dishes in larger quantities at a time and freezing them in the desired meal sizes in accordance with the methods and techniques I have developed over the last 52 years of experiments and trials without affecting either the taste or the flavour of the dishes. I am able to say that I am today in the happy position to have in my freezer a supply of ready made meals, which is enough to provide for me and my husband a good meal every day for three to four months, even if I did not do any cooking at all during all this period.

What quantity of any dish is to be cooked at a time would, of course, depend on the size of the family. For a couple the minimum quantity to be cooked should be such as to serve a total of four to six daily meals. Very often I now cook some dishes in a quantity which can be subdivided into 10 to 12 meals depending upon the dish we tend to relish more than the others. When the necessary preparatory work has been done, as explained earlier in this book, the time it would take to cook such a quantity of food would not be appreciably more than the time spent in cooking a single meal, but in the proposed larger measure the pot would produce the extra meals which can be enjoyed day after day for a number of days later out of the freezer!

For many years now my husband and I have been eating our daily meals taken out of our freezer cooked many weeks ago. Neither we nor any of the guests to whom we have served this food have found anything lacking in it either in taste or in flavour. My husband's mother came from a Mughal family of India and she was an expert in cooking the famous Mughlai style of food. Having eaten that food in his early years he has an established discriminating taste in his mouth of the best South Asian food. And for many years now he has been eating the food I have cooked coming out of our freezer day after day and has found it to be entirely acceptable to him in terms of his accustomed taste. Furthermore we have also obtained our nutrition and other benefits such as freedom from any health-wasting diseases and maintenance of moderate body weight over the many years we have been eating that food. Strangely enough, the food we take out of our freezer, when warmed up for eating, somehow tastes better and is perhaps hygienically safer than if we ate the food the same day on which it was cooked.

RECIPES

Many hundreds of years of experience and experimentation have given South Asian food such a degree of refinement and sophistication that a given recipe, by itself, is not enough to produce the desired results, unless there exists all the background knowledge of the practical methods and techniques involved in various stages of preparation and cooking. I have, for this reason, written extensively in the preceding sections of this book the procedures which are to be followed in the preparatory and operational stages. I suggest these should be carefully studied before any cooking is undertaken. The available books on South Asian recipes normally take the background knowledge of cooking for granted on the consideration that young women normally staying largely at home, as in the past, imbibed the unwritten background knowledge from their mothers or other elders. This has however, been missed out by the present generation of young women whose educational demand and priorities have left them little time to pay their full attention to the day to day cooking chores in the kitchen, and particularly to take note of the importance of the exercise of "eye judgement" and its concomitant "heat regulation", constantly involved in the cooking process which comes from background knowledge and cannot be expressed in a conventional recipe.

I should also mention that in the recipes the ingredients are listed only in their broad categories, so as to avoid repetition, and should be understood to mean wherever applicable, that the preparatory work upon them, common to many recipes, as explained in Chapters 2 and 3 has already been done. For instance the ingredient "meat," (means lamb or goat meat unless otherwise stated) listed in the recipes presupposes that the work of cutting the meat into suitable pieces called "boties" and of boiling and cleaning as explained in that chapter have been carried out. This also applies to the preparation of vegetables for cooking. The implementation of the preparatory actions should therefore be considered as an essential part of the recipes.

The recipes I have written are based on quantities enough to provide for one time main entree and a side dish good for two or at a stretch three persons. The real idea, however, is to cook at any one time a sufficient quantity of a dish which would provide a meal not only for the day but also for several more days through storage and freezing. Hence, the quantities shown in the recipes for individual ingredients should, in practice, be increased proportionately or judgementally according to the number of individual meals intended to be cooked.

I should also mention that the recipes included in this book are those for the standard food cooked on a day to day basis in South Asian homes. There are innumerable other dishes of specialities, both general and regional, for meat and vegetables and for desserts which are cooked from time to time in South Asian homes on festive or other religious and social occasions. Some of these specialties are, however, now fast becoming a part of the commercial fare in hotels and restaurants and they are undergoing constant changes to cater to a mixed clientele hailing from different South Asian regions.

The following explanations are offered with respect to some of the ingredients listed in the recipes.

MEAT:

Unless otherwise specified this should be understood to mean pieces of meat called "boties."

COMPOSITE MASALA:

This is my special combination of spices and other ingredients required for most of the curries. The various ingredients for this masala are listed on **page 16** for one pound of meat and should be proportionately adjusted when a smaller or larger quantity is cooked.

PEPPER:

Means the green hot pepper (not of the thin long size which is extra hot) of the medium size of the approximate length and thickness of one's little finger.

SALT:

About one teaspoon of salt is deemed adequate for one pound of meat but this can be adjusted according to one's taste requirement.

RED PEPPER:

Means the hot variety of dried pepper whole or ground and not cayenne which is not normally used in South Asian cooking.

TURMERIC

This should be bought in a powdered form sold in small containers from which it can be sprinkled out from the holes.

LEMON JUICE:

When fresh lemon is not available readymade real lemon juice may be used instead.

NON-VEGETARIAN DISHES

MEAT PIECES & POTATO CURRY
(Gravied)

Aloo Ka Salan

I lb. meat
I lb. potatoes (medium, cut into two
    halves)
I cup oil
I large onion, chopped
composite masala
½ cup fresh cilantro leaves

Fry chopped onion in oil on medium heat until golden brown. Pour half cup of water and cover pot for 1 minute. Uncover and stir onion. Add composite masala and half a cup of water and while stirring let simmering take place until masala becomes lumpy. Add meat and stir it well in lumpy masala. Then cover and on low heat, with sprinkles of water, and frequent stirring let meat cook in its moisture until it takes a dry look. Now continue process of bhoonna until oil collects around. Add 1 ½ cups of water and continue cooking on medium heat until meat turns some three-quarters tender. Add potatoes and enough water to stand about 2 inches above the substance. Cover and cook over high heat until water comes to boil for 2 or 3 minutes to have the potatoes turn soft. Reduce heat to low and let simmer for 2 or 3 minutes. Garnish with cilantro leaves, turn off heat for salan to achieve Dum as the heat slowly dies out.

MEAT PIECES & OKRA CURRY
(Gravied)

Bhindi Ka Salan

I lb. meat
I lb. okra (prepared, full length)
I cup oil
I large onion, chopped
composite masala
½ cup fresh cilantro leaves

Fry chopped onion in oil on medium heat until golden brown. Pour half cup of water and cover pot for 1 minute. Uncover and stir onion. Add composite masala and half a cup of water and while stirring let simmering take place until masala becomes lumpy. Add meat and stir it well in lumpy masala. Then cover and on low heat with sprinkles of water, and frequent stirring let meat cook in its moisture until it takes a dry look. Now continue process of bhoonna until oil collects around. Add 1 ½ cups of water and continue cooking on medium heat until meat turns some three quarters tender. Add okra and enough water to stand about 1 ½ inches above the substance. Cover and cook over high heat until water comes to boil for 2 or 3 minutes to be sure that okra has come up floating on the top. Reduce heat to low and let simmer for 2 or 3 minutes. Garnish with cilantro leaves, turn off heat for salan to achieve Dum as the heat slowly dies out.

MEAT PIECES & SQUASH CURRY
(Gravied)

Ghia Ka Salan

I lb. meat
I lb. squash, prepared
I cup oil
I large onion, chopped
composite masala
½ cup fresh cilantro leaves

Fry chopped onion in oil on medium heat until golden brown. Pour half cup of water and cover pot for 1 minute. Uncover and stir onion. Add composite masala and half cup of water and while stirring let simmering take place until masala becomes lumpy. Add meat and stir it well in lumpy masala. Then cover and on low heat, with sprinkles of water, and frequent stirring let meat cook in its moisture until it takes a dry look. Now continue process of bhoonna until oil collects around. Add 1 ½ cups of water and continue cooking on medium heat until meat turns some three quarters tender. Add prepared squash and about 2 ½ cups of water. Cover and cook over high heat until water comes to boil for 2 or 3 minutes. Reduce heat to low and let simmer for 5 or 6 minutes or more, checking out to see that the squash has turned soft. Garnish with cilantro leaves, turn off heat for salan to achieve Dum as the heat slowly dies out.

MEAT PIECES & TURNIP CURRY
(Gravied)

Shuljum Ka Salan

1 lb. meat
1 lb. turnips, prepared
1 cup oil
1 large onion, chopped
composite masala
½ cup fresh cilantro leaves

Fry chopped onion in oil on medium heat until golden brown. Pour half cup of water and cover pot for 1 minute. Uncover and stir onion. Add composite masala and half cup of water and while stirring let simmering take place until masala becomes lumpy. Add meat and stir it well in lumpy masala. Then cover and on low heat, with sprinkles of water, and frequent stirring let meat cook in its moisture until it takes a dry look. Now continue process of bhoonna until oil collects around. Add 1 ½ cups of water and continue cooking on medium heat until meat turns out some three quarters tender. Add prepared turnips and 2 cups of water. Cover and cook over high heat until water comes to boil for 2 or 3 minutes Reduce heat to low and let simmer for 2 or 3 minutes. Garnish with cilantro leaves, turn off heat for salan to achieve Dum as the heat slowly dies out.

MEAT PIECES & BEET CURRY
(Non-Gravied)
Choquander Ka Salan

I lb. meat
I lb. beet, prepared
I cup oil
I large onion, chopped
composite masala
1 cubic inch ginger - thinly sliced
2 green peppers (cut in small pieces)
½ cup fresh cilantro leaves

Fry chopped onion in oil on medium heat until golden brown. Pour half cup of water and cover for 1 minute. Add composite masala and half cup of water and while stirring let simmering take place until masala becomes lumpy. Add meat and stir it well in lumpy masala. Then cover and cook on low heat with sprinkles of water, and frequent stirring let meat cook in its moisture until it takes a dry look. Now continue process of bhoonna until oil collects around. Add beets, cover and continue cooking on low heat. The water released by the beet will cook both itself and also bring the meat to softness producing the desired non-gravied consistency in the salan. Garnish with ginger, green peppers and cilantro and turn off heat for salan to achieve Dum as the heat slowly dies out.

MEAT PIECES & ZUCCHINI CURRY
(Non-Gravied)
Torai Ka Salan

I lb. meat
I lb. zucchini, prepared
½ cup oil
2 large onions (semi finely chopped)
composite masala
2 green peppers (whole with stems)
½ cup fresh cilantro leaves

Fry one quarter of chopped onions in oil on medium heat until golden brown. Pour half cup of water and cover for 1 minute. Add composite masala and half cup of water and while stirring let simmering take place until masala becomes lumpy. Add meat and stir it well in lumpy masala. Then cover and on low heat, with sprinkles of water, and frequent stirring let meat cook in its moisture until it takes a dry look. Now continue with process of bhoonna until oil collects around. Add zucchini together with the remaining three quarters of chopped onion and cook on medium heat until meat turns tender and the desired non-gravied consistency of salan is obtained. Add whole green peppers with stems and let cook for a minute or two. Garnish with cilantro and turn off heat for salan to achieve Dum as the heat slowly dies out.

MEAT PIECES & CAULIFLOWER CURRY
(Non-Gravied)
Gobi Ka Salan

I lb. meat
I lb. cauliflower, prepared
I cup oil
1 large onion, chopped
composite masala
2 green peppers, sliced
½ cup cilantro leaves

Fry chopped onion in oil on medium heat until golden brown. Pour half cup of water and cover for 1 minute. Add composite masala and half cup of water and while stirring let simmering take place until masala becomes lumpy. Add meat and stir it well in lumpy masala. Then cover and cook on low heat with sprinkles of water, and frequent stirring let meat cook in its moisture until it takes a dry look. Now continue with process of bhoonna until oil collects around. Add cauliflower and continue cooking with sprinkles of water until meat turns tender and the desired consistency of salan is obtained. Garnish with peppers and cilantro and turn off heat for salan to achieve Dum as the heat slowly dies out.

MEAT PIECE & ONION CURRY
(Non-Gravied)
Ishto

I lb. meat
5 cloves
I large onion, chopped
I large cardamom
½ cup yogurt
¼ tsp. cumin seeds
I cup oil
I tsp. coriander, ground
5 cloves of garlic roughly chopped
5 black pepper corns, crushed
I cubic inch ginger, finely sliced
I tsp. coriander, ground
4 dry red peppers,
I large tomato, finely cut
broken into pieces
Salt to taste

Take two medium sized bowls. In bowl one mix finely cut tomatoes with yogurt. In bowl two put all the spice ingredients and salt and mix them well. Fry onion in oil on medium heat until brown. Add mixture of tomatoes and yogurt and cook on full heat until the liquid is thickened. Then add meat with all the spices and salt contained in bowl two. Cook on medium-low heat and let cooking take place stirring frequently until meat loses its moisture, turns tender and oil is released. Cover pot and reduce heat to low for some ten minutes and then turn off heat to permit Dum to take place as the heat dies out and the aroma is locked in.

MEAT PIECES & SPINACH CURRY
(Non-Gravied)

Palak Gosth Ka Salan

1 lb. meat
2 bunches spinach, chopped
¾ cup oil
1 large onion, chopped
composite masala
2 tbsp. dill weed, chopped
2 cups fresh cilantro leaves
2 green peppers, cut in small pieces

Fry chopped onion in oil on medium heat until golden brown. Add composite masala and half cup of water and let simmering take place until masala becomes lumpy. Add meat and stir it well in lumpy masala. Then cook on medium heat stirring from time to time until meat loses its moisture. Now continue with process of bhoonna until oil collects around. Add prepared spinach and dill weed and cook on low heat until water released by spinach is soaked up and meat becomes tender. Garnish with cilantro and green pepper. Cover and turn off heat for salan to achieve Dum as the heat dies out.

MEAT PIECES & CHANNA LENTIL CURRY
(Non-Gravied)

Channa Dal Ka Salan

1 lb. meat
1 lb. channa dal
¾ cup oil
1 large onion, chopped
composite masala — reduce salt to ½
  tsp.
2 green peppers — cut in small pieces
½ cup mint leaves — fresh or dry

Soak Channa dal with half a tsp. of salt in boiling water until the grains become fluffy and about one inch of water is left on top. Set aside. Fry chopped onion in oil on medium heat until golden brown. Add composite masala and half cup of water and let simmering take place until masala becomes lumpy. Add meat and stir it well in lumpy masala. Then cook on medium heat stirring from time to time until meat loses its moisture. Now continue with process of bhoonna until oil collects around. Add soaked up channa dal with the water left on the top and cook on low heat until meat becomes tender and Channa dal is softened. Garnish with mint leaves and green pepper. Cover and turn off heat for salan to achieve Dum as the heat dies out.

GROUND MEAT & CAULIFLOWER CURRY
(Non-Gravied)

Gobi Ka Salan

I lb. ground meat
2 green peppers, sliced
I lb. cauliflower - florets only
I large tomato, chopped
¾ cup oil
I tsp. red pepper, ground
I large onion, chopped
  I tsp. salt (or to taste)
2 tsp. yogurt
½ cup fresh coriander leaves
I tbsp. garlic/ginger paste
I tsp. coriander, crushed
I" cube ginger — thinly sliced

Fry chopped onion in oil on medium heat until golden brown. Add garlic/ginger paste, chopped tomato and yogurt mixed together and proceed with process of bhoonna until oil is separated. Add ground meat, coriander, red pepper and salt and put on high heat. Proceed again with the process of bhoonna until meat has released its moisture. Now add cauliflower, green peppers and sliced ginger and mixing them well, cover pot and leave on high heat for 5 minutes or so. Then turn off heat and garnish with coriander leaves and Dum will be achieved as the heat dies out.

GROUND MEAT & POTATO & PEAS CURRY
(Non-Gravied)

Keema Aloo/Matar Ka Salan

I lb. ground meat
1" cube ginger, thinly sliced
I lb. potatoes, diced
2 green peppers, cut in small pieces
¾ cup oil
½ lb. green peas
1 large tomato, chopped
1 large onion, chopped
1 tsp. red pepper, ground (or as per taste)
2 tsp. yogurt
I tbsp. garlic/ginger paste
1 tsp. salt or as per taste
I tsp. coriander, crushed
1 cup fresh cilantro leaves

Fry chopped onion in oil on medium heat until golden brown. Add garlic/ginger paste, chopped tomatoes and yogurt mixed together and proceed with process of bhoonna until oil is separated. Add ground meat, coriander and red pepper and salt and on high heat continue process of bhoonna until meat has released its moisture. Now add diced potatoes, peas, green pepper and sliced ginger and stirring all contents cover pot and leave on high heat for 5 minutes or so. Then garnish with cilantro leaves, turn off heat for salan to achieve Dum as the heat dies out.

GROUND MEAT & BITTER MELON CURRY
(Non-Gravied)

Karela Ka Salan

1 lb. ground meat
I" cube ginger, thinly sliced
1 lb. bitter melon, prepared sliced
¾ cup oil
2 green peppers, (cut in ½ finely cut)
3 large onions, (2 ½ chopped, small pieces)
1 large tomato, chopped
2 tsp. yogurt
1 tsp. red pepper, ground
1 tbsp. garlic/ginger paste
1 tsp. salt (or as per taste)
1 tsp. coriander, crushed
I cup fresh cilantro leaves
I sprinkle turmeric

STAGE I

Smooth out outer skin of bitter melons with a peeler and slicing across in two parts remove the seeds and take them out of their pockets discarding the latter. Apply salt on bitter melon shells and seeds and leave them to soak for two or three hours. Then wash them thoroughly removing all salt and leave them in a colander to dry. Later dry them still further by wrapping each shell in paper towels and set them aside with the seeds.

STAGE II

Fry onion in oil on medium heat until about half brown. Add chopped tomato, ginger/garlic paste, crushed coriander, yogurt and one sprinkle of turmeric. Carry out process of bhoonna until oil is separated.

Now add ground meat and cook on medium heat until meat has released its moisture. Garnish the cooked meat with a mixture of chopped cilantro leaves and finely cut onion.

STAGE III

Now fill the bitter melon shells (previously kept aside in paper towels) with part of the cooked meat from Stage II and tie up the shells tightly around with sewing thread and set them aside. Fry the seeds in oil on medium heat until they are browned. Take the seeds out and with some extra oil fry the bitter melon shells as wrapped, turning them around until they too take a uniform brown look. Now spread the fried seeds in the cooked meat mixing them well in the meat and lay out on the top in an orderly way the bound filled bitter melon shells, pouring on them the oil remaining in the frying pan. Add a sprinkle of water and cook on low heat until shells are softened and oil has collected around. Garnish with cilantro leaves and finely cut ginger and cover pot for salan to achieve Dum as the heat dies out.

MEAT CURRY SIMPLE
Sada Salan

I lb. meat
½ cup oil
I large onion, chopped
composite masala
½ cup fresh cilantro leaves

Fry chopped onion in oil until golden brown. Pour half cup of water and cover pot for one minute. Uncover and stir contents. Add composite masala and a cup of water and stir on medium heat until masala becomes lumpy. Add meat and on medium low heat, putting sprinkles of water, proceed with process of bhoonna until meat turns soft. Add additional amount of water to the level of liquid desired in the curry. As the golden colour oil begins to float on the top, cover the pot and open the burner to full heat for a minute and then, garnishing with cilantro leaves, turn heat off for salan to achieve Dum as the heat slowly dies out.

MEAT CURRY CLASSICAL
Korma Mughlai

I lb. meat
4 small cardamoms
I ½ cup yogurt
4 cloves
I cup oil
¼ tsp. saffron
3 medium onions, finely chopped
I cubic inch ginger, finely cut
2 tbsp. ginger-garlic paste
I tsp. garam masala
I tsp. cumin seeds
I tsp. ground red pepper (or 4 black pep-
    percorns to taste)
4 tbsp. kewra (screw pine essence)
1 tsp. salt (or as per taste)

Fry chopped onion in oil until golden brown. Take out browned onion in a bowl and set aside for later use. Put garam masala in heated oil and after a few seconds add meat pieces and salt and mix with a large spoon. Add ginger-garlic paste and proceed with the process of bhoonna until meat turns pinkish brown. Add ground red pepper and continue bhoonna until meat loses its moisture. Add some water to have meat turn tender on low heat. Now, in a bowl blend together golden fried onions previously set aside with yogurt, cardamoms, cloves, cumin seeds, black peppers and saffron. Add this blended mixture to the meat and again carry out process of bhoonna until oil begins to be released. Then add a quarter cup of water and cook on full heat for a few minutes. Now spread the finely cut ginger and kewra and leave on low heat for a few minutes. Then turn off heat and allow Dum to take place as the heat slowly dies out.

MEAT (SHANK) CURRY
Nahari

5 lb. shank
(Spices/Masala)*
2 large onions, finely chopped
4 cloves
1 large garlic bulb, finely chopped
1 cardamom, large
2 cups oil
20 cardamoms, small
4 tbsp. wheat flour
2 tsp. cumin seeds
4 tsp. garlic, chopped
6" cinnamon stick
2 cups fennel
3 bay leaves, large size
2 tsp. red pepper, ground
I nutmeg seed
 (or as per taste)

I tbsp. mace
I cup fresh cilantro leaves
I ½ tsp. black pepper
I tbsp. salt (or as per taste)

Take cooking of this dish in several steps.

Step I.
Put wheat flour and fennel in oven at 300 degrees and brown them, turning them from time to time. Then mix well both fennel and flour and add the ground red pepper. Grind all spices listed under the column* as finely as possible in a coffee grinder and pass it further through a fine mesh sifter to reduce it to a powder. Now mix all these ingredients together and keep them fully covered.

Step II.
Have shank deboned by a butcher and after removing any fat and loose membranes have it sliced across in two parts without fraying the inside muscle. Also have the shank bones cut into about l ½ inch size parts and obtain from the butcher an equal quantity of additional marrow bones of the same size.

Step III.
To start cooking place all bones at the bottom of the pot and lay the shanks on top of them sprinkling on some salt. Add 8 cups of water and bring to boil. As the meat turns some ¾ soft take it out of the pot and cleaning it further of any sticking membranes, cut the shanks with a sharp knife into small pieces about l ½" cubes without fraying the ends. Also take out the bones from the pot and extract their marrow in a dish and put it aside. The liquid or the broth left in the pot is called Yakhni.

Step IV.
Warm the oil and add all the combined masala (Step I) and cover immediately for a minute to preserve flavor. Now add the Yakhni and put in the shank meat pieces previously cut such that the liquid in the pot is some 2 inches above the meat. Cover the pot and on low heat allow cooking to take place without coming to boil for an hour or so until the meat turns soft.

Step V.
Fry chopped onion in oil until golden brown and then add to it chopped garlic, and as it turns brown, transfer them together with the oil into the pot.

Step VI.
Now warm the bone marrow previously set aside (Step III) and sprinkling over it some salt and ground pepper pour over it some melted butter and turn off heat to prevent any melting of the marrow. Then spread the marrow on the top of the cooked meat and leave the pot on very low heat for a minute or two. At the time of eating garnish with cilantro leaves.

MEAT BALLS CURRY
Koftay

2 lb. ground meat
PREPARATION OF GRAVY
2 large onions, chopped
1 cup oil
3 ½ tsp. coriander, ground
2 tbsp. ginger-garlic paste
1 tsp. red pepper, ground
1 tsp. salt or as per taste

PREPARATION OF MEAT BALLS
1 medium onion, finely chopped
¾ cup yogurt
½ tsp. coriander, ground
2 green peppers, chopped
1 cup cilantro leaves, chopped
1 tsp. roasted chick peas, ground
½ tsp. rice powder
I tsp. salt, or as per taste
½ tsp. garam masala

Gravy

Fry chopped onion in oil on medium heat until golden brown. Pour one cup of water and cover pot for one minute. Uncover and stir onions. Add coriander ground, ginger and garlic paste, red pepper ground, salt and one cup of water and let cooking take place on medium heat until masala becomes lumpy. Add again one cup of water and bring to a boil and then shut off heat leaving the gravy in a semi-liquid state.

Meat Balls

Now start preparation of meat balls. The first step is to put ground meat in a food processor and mince it to a dough like state. Take the meat out in a bowl and add ground roasted chick peas, garam masala, ground red pepper, ground coriander, chopped cilantro leaves, chopped green pepper, medium onion, finely chopped and salt and mix all these ingredients thoroughly with the minced meat. Then add ¾ of the yogurt and on medium heat with sprinkles of water bring meat into a semi-soft malleable state. Now divide the meat into equal portions and roll each portion with both palms of hands into round balls about the size of a golf ball. Put all the meat balls so made on a tray and gently lay them in the pot one by one into the lumpy liquid gravy mentioned above in the pot. Now in a bowl put the remaining yogurt, cilantro, green pepper, chopped onion, and mix up them well. Spread this mixture over the meat balls in the pot. Cover pot and on medium heat let cooking take place for some 15 minutes or so. Then pick up the pot from the burner once or twice and roll it gently around so that the meat balls are well soaked in the gravy. The koftay will be ready when they are well surrounded and covered with the gravy.

This dish can be enriched by adding peeled rounded turnips slightly fried in oil and put into the pot at the time the meat balls previously put in have begun to firm up. The dish would then be called Shab-Deg.

GROUND MEAT KEBABS
Shami Kebabs

*2 lb. ground meat

*2 ½ tbsp. Channa Dal (pre-soaked in
   water for 1 hour)

*4 dry red peppers, whole

*2 medium onions, cut in small pieces

*2 tsp. poppy seeds (khus-khus)

*salt, to taste

**½ cup fresh cilantro leaves, finely cut

**2 green peppers, finely chopped

**½ medium onion, crushed, juiced out

**I tsp. garam masala

**2 tsp. rice powder

**I lemon — grated rind only

I large egg

Put together in a pot all one-starred ingredients and add two and a half full cups of water. Mix well. On high heat bring water to boil. Cover and let cook, stirring from time to time, until all moisture has evaporated. Then transfer the meat onto a large steel plate to be well aired and cooled. Now put the meat into a food processor and grind it finely. Then taking the meat out of the processor put in both the white and the yolk of the egg and mix thoroughly. Now add all the remaining double-starred ingredients and mix them well. Shape the meat compound into patties in round sizes about half the size of a hamburger. In a heavy-bottom frying pan heat the oil and then on medium heat deep fry the meat patties until they are brown on both sides. Place the fried patties on a paper towel to absorb the oil. When serving (if cold) the patties should be heated in a toaster oven. The kebabs not needed for early use should be kept in the refrigerator for some 12 hours and then transferred into the freezer in a large plastic container, each layer of kebabs separated from the other by wax paper.

SKEWERED KEBAB*
Seekh Kebab

2 lb. ground meat

2 large onions, chopped

10 small cardamoms, seeded

3 large cardamoms, seeded

1 tbsp. roasted chick peas, ground

2 tsp. ground red pepper

2 tsp. dry pomegranate seeds

1 tsp. mace

1 nutmeg seed

¾ tsp. black pepper corns

1 inch cinnamon stick, broken in pieces

2 bay leaves

salt, to taste

Fry onion in oil on medium heat, until golden brown. Now take onion out and spread it on a kitchen towel to drain out oil. Grind all other ingredients to fine powder in a coffee grinder. Spread this ground powder over the ground meat in a bowl and mix thoroughly. Now crush the fried onion well and spread it over the meat and mix it thoroughly. Divide the meat in portions sufficient to roll each portion about 6 inches long and 1 ½ inches in circumference. For barbequing the rolls follow the instructions as noted under the heading of the recipe.

---

* Note: these kebabs are barbequed but instead of using skewers the same effect is produced by passing the handle of a wooden spoon through a six inch long roll of meat slightly tapered at both ends and then taking the handle out and leaving a ½" tunnel inside the roll so as to cook the kebabs from inside. The rolls are then placed side by side on the barbeque grill and at a low temperature cooked to golden brown all around.

WHOLE CHICKEN CURRY
Murghi ka Salan

2 lb. chicken pieces
I ½" fresh ginger, chopped
I cup oil
3 medium onions, chopped
6 small cardamoms, broken at one end
6 tbsp. yogurt
I ½ tbs. garlic-ginger paste
3 green peppers, each cut in three pieces
3 tsp. coriander, ground
I tsp. red pepper, ground
1 cup cilantro leaves
salt, as per taste

Have two medium size bowls ready and use them as follows:

Bowl # 1.

Put in this bowl chicken pieces and spread on top of them garlic/ginger paste, chopped ginger and cardamoms one side broken.

Bowl # 2.

Put in this bowl, yogurt, coriander ground, red pepper ground, green pepper pieces, salt and about 1 ½ cup of water and set aside.

Fry chopped onion in oil on medium heat until about ¾ browned and then empty in it contents of bowl # 1 and mix well. Then proceed with the process of bhoonna until chicken pieces cease sticking to the pot. Now empty in this the contents of bowl #2 and bring it to boil for about 5 minutes. Then reduce heat and let cooking go on until chicken becomes tender and the desired amount of liquid (shurwa) is left on the top. Garnish with cilantro, turn off heat and cover pot for Dum to be achieved.

RICE WITH MEAT
Biryani, Classical

3 lb. meat

2 lb. rice

Ingredients - Stage I

4 tbsp. coriander, whole

1 large garlic whole, unpeeled

4" ginger, lightly crushed

6 cloves

6 black peppers

1 tbsp. cumin seeds

3 cardamom, large

l tbsp. kevra (Screw pine essence)

salt, to taste

Ingredients - Stage II

1 large onion, chopped

1 garlic, whole, peeled

6 cardamoms, small

2" ginger, finely cut

1 cup yogurt

½ cup oil

1 tsp. saffron

Note: Make a bag of thin cotton fabric, 10" long, 4" wide, sewing a l" wide cavity pocket at the opening and putting a cord through it such that the bag can be opened and closed by passing the cord through it. This bag, after use, should be washed, throughly dried and stored for future use.

STAGE I

Fill loosely in the bag described in note all the spices listed under the heading, Ingredients — Stage I, and lay the bag at the bottom of the pot in which the cooking is to be done. Place the meat on the top of the bag and add three glasses of water. Let cooking of the meat take place on medium heat until the meat becomes ¾ tender. Then using a colander drain out the liquid in a bowl and squeeze out firmly into the bowl all the spice juices from the bag throwing out the juiced out spices. The liquid so obtained is called Yakhni. Keep this yakhni and the meat aside and now proceed to the next stage of cooking.

STAGE II

From the list of spices listed under the heading — Ingredients — Stage II — blend the unpeeled garlic in ½ cup of water. Pass it through a fine sieve and keep the resulting spice liquid aside.

Now fry chopped onion in oil on medium heat until it is slightly browned. Now add to it the garlic juice from stage II and on medium heat let the liquid evaporate. Add yogurt and also let its liquid evaporate. Now adding ginger and cardamoms proceed with the process of bhoonna until oil is separated. Add yakhni prepared under stage I and bring it to boil.

THE FINAL STAGE

If all the Biryani is to be cooked immediately, then add rice, previously thoroughly washed, and cook on medium heat until all the moisture has evaporated. Then spread the saffron and the kewra essence on the top.

Now pre-heat the oven to full strength and then shut it off. Place the Biryani pot in the oven shutting the oven door. In about 15 minuets, Dum will be achieved and the rice will puff up as the oven heat dies out.

CONSERVATION & STORAGE

Under the system of cooking I am proposing, I should like to suggest that the quantity of yakhni and the meat be such as to allow at least 5 or 6 portions to be made, each a meal for 2 persons, for freezing for future use. In such a case the yakhni and the meat prepared under Stage I and II should be frozen together in individual cartons in the proportion of 6 pieces of meat to about 2 ½ cups of yakhni. When defrosted this will take about l ½ cups of rice duly washed to complete the Biryani dish.

BIRYANI MUGHLAI

2 lbs. rice
½ cup milk
2 ½ lbs. meat
6 small cardamoms, ends broken
4 tbsp. yogurt
I tsp. saffron
I tsp. salt, or as per taste
I tsp. kevra (screw pine essence)

First cook Korma (meat curry Mughlai as described in a separate recipe) and keep aside. Boil rice until it becomes soft from outside and a little hard at the core called <u>kani</u>. In a separate pot make a layer of rice. Now mix yogurt and saffron in the Korma (previously cooked as mentioned above), make a layer of a part of gravy and meat in a separate pot and spread a portion of rice over it. Again make a second layer of another part gravy and meat and spread another portion of rice over it. Repeat this for the third time using up the remaining one-third of gravy and meat and the rice. Allow the cooking of this combination of rice and meat to take place on very low heat for a few minutes to have the two components absorbed into each other. In a cup of milk add the cardamom, saffron and the kewra and mixing well transfer them into the pot, still leaving it on the burner for two or three minutes and then turning off heat for the Biryani to achieve Dum as the heat dies out.

FISH CURRY
Muchli ka Salan

2 salmon steaks ½" thick (substitute any
   fish - steak cut)
2 large onions - finely cut
1 cup oil
¾ cup yogurt
½ tsp. red pepper, ground
1 tsp. coriander, ground
1 tsp. ginger-garlic paste
1 tsp. dry methi, leaves (fenugreek)*
1 tsp. salt or as per taste
1/4 tsp. turmeric powder

Rub fish steak with salt and turmeric making sure it penetrates fish. Fry onion in oil on medium heat until brown. Add methi. Make mixture of garlic/ginger paste, red pepper and coriander with a small amount of yogurt, add this mixture to the browned onion and proceed with the process of bhoonna until oil is separated and bubbles appear. For added flavour carry on with bhoonna on very low heat for another 5 minutes. The masala is now ready. Add salt to taste. Now add fish after washing it thoroughly and cover it all around with masala. Cover pot and leave it on low heat to simmer for some 10 minutes. Then shut off heat and allow Dum to be achieved as the heat dies out.

*Normally available in Asian food shops.

VEGETARIAN DISHES

LONG SQUASH
Draz Ghia ki subzi

I squash of medium length and thickness
2 tbsp. oil
I tbsp. lemon juice
½ tsp. ground red pepper
½ tsp. cumin seeds
½ cups fresh cilantro leaves
salt as per taste

Fry cumin seeds in oil on low heat for four to five minutes. Add squash, peeled and cut into pieces about an inch long and half inch wide, and cover on medium heat. As the squash is cooked to softness add pepper, lemon juice and salt. Stir and cover again for three to four minutes. Garnish with cilantro leaves, cover pot and turn off heat for subzi to achieve Dum as the heat dies out.

ROUND SQUASH
Meethe Ghia ki subzi

2 lb. squash
½ tsp. cumin seeds
I cup oil
½ cup fresh cilantro leaves
2 medium onions, cut in small pieces
2 tsp. lemon juice
4 dry red peppers, broken in 3 pieces each
½ tsp. cumin seeds
¼ tsp. turmeric powder
salt as per taste

Peel the squash of its thick skin and cut into pieces about one inch square. Put this in a large bowl and pouring lemon juice over it set aside. Now fry onion in oil over medium heat until it is slightly browned. Add the squash pieces and sprinkle over it the cumin seeds, pepper and turmeric and stir well. Cover and let cooking take place on medium heat until squash turns soft and all moisture has evaporated. Garnish with cilantro leaves, cover pot and turn off heat for subzi to achieve Dum as the heat dies out.

ZUCCHINI
Torai ki subzi

2 lb. zucchini
I cup oil
2 medium onions, chopped
4 dry red peppers,
 cut into some 4 pieces each
I cubic inch ginger, crushed
2 tbsp. lemon oil
¼ tsp. turmeric
½ cup cilantro leaves
salt as per taste

Peel zucchini as explained earlier and cut it into about ¼ inch thick round pieces. Fry chopped onion in oil on medium heat until about half brown. Add zucchini and top it with pepper, ginger, lemon juice and turmeric. Cover and let cooking take place on medium heat until zucchini turns soft and liquid has evaporated. Garnish with cilantro leaves, cover pot and turn off heat for subzi to achieve Dum as the heat dies out.

EGG PLANT
Baigan ki subzi

I lb. egg plant
I large potato, cut into ½ inch square
 pieces
I medium onion, cut into small pieces
I large tomato, sliced like onion rounds
I cubic inch ginger, chopped
2 garlic cloves, chopped
2 dry whole red peppers, cut into two or
 three pieces each
½ tsp. red pepper, ground
I tsp. cumin seeds
½ cup oil
½ cup fresh cilantro leaves
I piece mango pickle
salt as per taste

Fry cumin seeds in oil on low heat until they look golden. Add whole red pepper and allow it to turn blackish. Now add all other ingredients except cilantro and lemon juice and stir them for a while keeping cover in hand to protect against any sparking out from the pot. Allow cooking to take place on medium heat. When all moisture has evaporated, add lemon juice and the piece of mango pickle along with a bit of oil from the pickle. Cover for five minutes and see if the oil has collected around. If not, add a small quantity of oil and cover again for a few minutes. Garnish with cilantro, cover and turn off heat for the subzi to achieve Dum as the heat slowly dies out.

OKRA
Bhindi ki subzi

1 lb. okra
2 medium onions, chopped
l/3 cup oil
2 tbsp. lemon juice
4 dry red peppers, cut in small pieces
1 green pepper, chopped
½ tsp cumin seeds
½ cup cilantro leaves
¼ tsp. turmeric powder
salt, as per taste

Prepare okra and cut it in ¾ inch pieces horizontally. In a bowl pour lemon juice over cut pieces of okra and shake well. Fry onion in oil on medium heat until slightly browned. Add okra pieces and top them with pepper, cumin seeds and turmeric and mix well. Cover and let cooking take place on medium heat until okra turns soft and all moisture has evaporated. Garnish with cilantro, cover pot and turn off heat for Dum to be achieved as the heat dies out.

SPINACH & POTATOES
Palak aloo ki subzi

1 large bunch of spinach
1 large potato, cut into about ¾" cubes
1 medium onion, chopped
3 dry red peppers, broken in small parts
1 tsp. cumin seeds
1" cubic inch ginger, chopped
½ cup fresh cilantro leaves
¼ tsp. turmeric powder
salt, as per taste

Wash spinach thoroughly and dry it in a colander. Then holding a bunch of it tightly in your hand cut it in reasonably fine pieces. Fry onion along with red pepper in oil on medium heat. When the onion turns to pink in colour add the spinach, sprinkling over it the turmeric and putting in the salt and cover quickly. After a minute or two uncover and add the potatoes and let cooking take place on medium heat until the potatoes have turned soft and no liquid is left. Cover again on very low heat for one or two minutes. Garnish with cilantro and turn off heat for the subzi to achieve Dum as the heat dies out.

Meat Pieces & Cauliflower Curry *(Pg.28)*

Rice With Meat *(Pg.37)*

Meat Pieces & Turnip Curry *(Pg.26)*

Meat Pieces & Potato Curry *(Pg.25)*

Fish Curry *(Pg.38)*

Yellow Lentil *(Pg.49)*

Spinach & Potatoes *(Pg.42)*

Okra *(Pg.42)*

Cauliflower, Peas & Potatoes *(Pg.43)*

Rice & Channa Dal *(Pg.48)*

Semolina Halwa *(Pg.53)*

Sweet Rice *(Pg.52)*

CAULIFLOWER, PEAS & POTATOES
Gobi, matar, aloo ki subzi

I whole cauliflower
2 medium potatoes
½ lb. peas, shelled
I cubic inch ginger, finely cut
I tsp. cumin seeds
2 green hot peppers, cut in small pieces
2 dry red peppers, broken in small pieces
I medium onion, cut in small pieces
2 tsp. lemon juice
6 garlic cloves, cut in small pieces
½ cup oil
½ cup fresh cilantro leaves
¼ tsp. turmeric powder
salt to taste

In a large pan fry cumin seeds, green and red pepper in oil at very low heat for some five minutes. Add cauliflower and potatoes as cut, and top it up with onion, ginger, turmeric powder and salt and mix them well. Cover and cook on low heat, stirring from time to time keeping flowers intact until potatoes turn soft. Add peas and cover pan for some five minutes keeping heat very low and then garnish with cilantro and turn off heat for the subzi to achieve Dum as the heat dies out.

Note: Carefully separate the flowers from the cauliflower. Peel the stem and cut the pith into small florets. Cut the potatoes into about half inch squares.

SPINACH & RAPINI
Sag ki subzi

1 packet frozen spinach
1 bunch rapini, fresh
2 green peppers, finely cut
3 cubic inch ginger, cut and chopped
2 whole garlic, peeled and chopped
5 cloves garlic, chopped
¼ tsp. turmeric
salt to taste
½ cup fresh cilantro leaves

Frozen spinach should be preferred to fresh spinach. This is to save time taken in washing off any soil sticking to fresh leaves. Rapini is not normally available in frozen packaging. The rapini should be thoroughly washed and then the skin from its stem extending to its leaves should be peeled. Both spinach and rapini bunches should then be held in hand lengthwise and cut across in small pieces.

Put the spinach and the rapini in a pot and top it with green peppers, ginger, garlic, turmeric and salt and 10 cups of water. Allow cooking to take place on full heat until all water has evaporated and the spinach and rapini have taken a pulp-like form. Garnish with cilantro, turn off heat leaving the pot on the burner to achieve Dum as the heat dies out.

This dish needs a *baghar*, namely, it needs to be topped at the end with a charge of 4 or 5 chopped cloves of garlic fried to golden colour in three or four tablespoons of oil. Spread the oil and the fried garlic pieces on the top of the cooked spinach and rapini and cover the pot quickly to lock up the flavour. The dish is now ready for eating.

BITTER MELON & CHANNA DAL
Karela Channa Dal ki subzi

I lb. bitter melon
I cup channa dal
I large tomato, cut in small pieces
I medium onion, chopped
½ cup oil
I ½ tsp. coriander ground
I ½ tsp. garlic-ginger paste
2 dry red peppers, broken in small pieces
½ tsp. turmeric
salt to taste
½ cup fresh cilantro leaves

Peel the bitter melon to smoothness and then cut it across, recovering the seeds and throwing away the fluff. Take the seeds out of their pockets and cut the karela skin into strips about one inch long and half inch wide. Put the karela strips and the seeds in a bowl and mixing them with about one tablespoonful of salt set them aside for about an hour. Thereafter, wash the karela strips and the seeds thoroughly to remove the salt and a deep fry in oil on medium heat until they are golden brown.

Now wash the channa dal in hot water and putting it in a pot and adding two cups of water and salt to taste bring it to boil.

Then in the oil remaining after the karela strips and seeds have been deep fried add chopped onion, ginger or garlic paste, coriander, and tomato and proceed with the process of bhoonna until the oil swims up. Now add the channa dal along with the water in which it has been boiled and the fried karela strips, and seeds and on medium heat let cooking take place until the channa dal has turned soft and the water has evaporated. Garnish with cilantro and turn off heat for Dum to be achieved as the heat dies out.

OPTIONAL

These subzis can be made more *chatpatti* (spicy hot) by adding about half a teaspoonful of Chat Masala along with other spices listed in the recipes.

RICE & LENTIL DISHES

PLAIN RICE
Khushka

I lb. rice

¼ bar butter

Wash rice thoroughly in hot water. Bring about 6 cups of water to boil and add to it the washed rice. (Leave a spoon inside the pot to prevent spilling out of water.) When the rice is cooked to about ¾ or more of its softness take it out in a colander and drain out the water. Now pour some cold water upon the rice to clean out any accumulated starch. Transfer the cleaned rice into a Corningware dish topping it with the butter. At eating time, place the rice dish in the microwave oven for some five minutes. The rice will fluff up and will be ready to eat as it is brought to the dining table steaming hot.

RICE & RED LENTIL
Khichri Masoor ki Dal

I lb. rice
I lb. red lentil
½ cup oil
I small onion, chopped
2 red peppers dry —
   broken in two-three pieces
I tbsp. butter (about ¼ bar)
I tsp. salt or as per taste
(Best when cooked some 45 minutes
   before eating)

In a bowl wash together rice and lentil thoroughly in warm water and set aside. Fry chopped onion, with red pepper pieces, in oil on medium heat until lightly browned. Add rice and lentil and put in enough water to stand about an inch on the top. Add salt and stir the contents once or twice. Add butter. Bring to boil on full heat for two or three minutes not allowing to overflow. Then reduce heat to medium and continue cooking until all water has evaporated and small holes form on the surface. Stir again, cover and leave pot on lowest heat for some 20 minutes to achieve Dum as the heat dies out.

RICE & CHANNA DAL
Qubuli

2 cups rice
½ cup oil
I cup channa dal
½ bar butter
I medium onion, chopped
4 black peppers (m)
I large cardamom (m)
½ tsp. cumin seeds (m)
½ tsp. garlic powder (m)
I tsp. salt or as per taste (m)

Wash rice thoroughly in warm water and set aside. Wash channa dal in hot water and let it remain soaked in that water for about an hour. Fry onion in oil on medium heat until mid brown. Now add all masala ingredients marked letter (m), first mixing them in a small amount of water in a bowl and stirring them with onion until the garlic smell is removed and oil is released. Now add channa dal drained of its water. Pour 2 cups of water and on full heat bring it to boil. Then cover pot and keeping heat low check from time to time until dal has turned halfway soft. Add rice and stirring it gently add two cups of water and on full heat bring it to boil. Now reduce heat to low for 5 minutes and then turn it off for Qubuli to achieve Dum as the heat dies out.

RICE & POTATOES
Tahari

I lb. rice
I large potato, diced
½ cup oil
I medium onion, chopped
½ bar butter
½ tsp. granulated garlic (m)
I inch cube fresh ginger, finely cut (m)
I inch cinnamon stick, cut in two (m)
4 each cloves and black pepper (m)
½ tsp. cumin seeds (m)
I large cardamom (m)
½ tsp. ground red pepper (m)
I small green pepper, cut in two (m)
1 tsp. salt or as per taste (m)

Fry onion in oil on medium heat until mid brown. Add all masala ingredients marked with letter (m), mixing them in a small amount of water and keep stirring with sprinkles of water until garlic smell is removed and oil is released. Now add diced potatoes and stir them in the masala with a small amount of water. Cover the pot and let cooking take place for a few minutes. Add rice with about 2 ½ cups of water and stir all contents. Cover and on high heat allow water to come to boil. Now add butter and stir again. Cover and leave on low heat for 5 minutes. Then turn off heat and allow Dum to be achieved as the heat dies out.

YELLOW LENTIL
Arhar ki dal

1 lb. dal arhar
1 small onion, finely chopped
2 dry red peppers,
  each broken in 2 pieces
2 tbsp. oil
¼ tsp. turmeric
1 tbsp. lemon juice
salt, as per taste

Wash lentil thoroughly and then soak it in hot water for about an hour. Then put lentil in the pot and add two cups of water. Put salt and red peppers and sprinkle the turmeric. On high heat bring water to boil and then on low heat let cooking go on without any stirring, until the lentil is softened. Then reduce the lentil to pulp by crushing with a spoon. Add lemon juice and mix well.

BAGHAR

Fry chopped onion on medium heat in oil to golden colour and top the lentil with it, covering the pot and turning off heat to achieve Dum as the heat dies out.

RED LENTIL
Masoor ki dal

1 lb. masoor dal
1 small onion, chopped
2 tbsp. oil
2 dry red peppers, broken in pieces
salt to taste
¼ tsp. turmeric
salt, to taste
l tbsp. lemon juice

Wash lentil thoroughly and transfer to the pot with two cups of water. Add salt and red pepper and sprinkle turmeric on top. Bring water to boil and let cooking take place until lentil turns soft. Now add lemon juice and mix well and keep pot on very low heat.

BAGHAR

Fry onion in oil on medium heat and until golden brown, top the lentil with it and covering the pot, turn off heat to achieve Dum as the heat dies out.

BLACK LENTIL
Kali Masoor Dal

1 lb. black lentil
2 medium onions, chopped
2 tbsp. oil
I cup yogurt
2 tbsp. coriander, ground
I tsp. red pepper, ground
2 tsp. lemon juice
I tsp. turmeric
½ cup fresh or dry mint leaves
5 cloves fresh garlic, finely chopped
salt, to taste

Wash lentil thoroughly and let it soak in hot water for a good one hour. Bring four cups of water to boil and then put lentil in it along with coriander, pepper, turmeric, chopped onion and salt. Let cooking take place on medium heat until lentil turns soft. Add yogurt and lemon juice and mix them thoroughly into the lentil with an electric mixer until the mixture turns soft. Leave pot on very low heat.

BAGHAR

Fry chopped garlic in oil on medium heat until it turns golden brown and then transfer the fried garlic and the oil on to the lentil pot. Cover for a minute to lock in the flavour. Uncover and spread mint leaves around into the pot. Turn off heat for cooked lentil to achieve Dum as the heat dies out.

DESSERTS

SWEET RICE
Zarda (Simple)

I lb. rice
I cup sugar
¼ cup raisins
¼ cup sliced almonds
¼ cup pistachios, shelled
½ tsp. food colouring, yellow

Boil 4 cups of water with colour added. Wash rice thoroughly and put it in the boiled water. Let rice cook to about ¾ softness and then take it out in a colander and let it drain and dry for about three hours. Then put rice back again in the pot and add sugar, sliced almonds, and pistachios and let cooking take place on medium heat until water released by sugar has fully evaporated. Now fry raisins in a small amount of butter until they are fluffed up and spread them over the cooked rice. Leave pot covered for a few minutes and turn off heat for Dum to be achieved.

SWEET RICE
Zarda (Mughlai)

I lb. rice
¾ cup sugar
½ cup oil
2 tbsp. almonds, sliced
3 tbsp. pistachios, shelled
¼ cup raisins
4 cardamoms, small
¼ tsp. saffron
I tbsp. kewra (screw pine essence)

Wash rice thoroughly and soak it in water. Also soak raisins until fluffed up. Fill four cups of water in a pot and add in it the sugar and the saffron and bring it to boil. Now after fully draining out the water from the soaked rice put it back into the pot and let cooking take place on low heat until all moisture has evaporated. Now cover the pot with a heavy lid or put on a heavy object on the lid to lock in flavour and lower heat to the minimum for approx. 15 minutes

Now in a frying pan fry the cardamoms in oil until they turn lightly brown. Then take out the cardamom and lightly fry in the same oil the sliced almonds and the pistachios and the raisins. Thereafter transfer them all to the pot with the kewra essence and cover pot again with a heavy lid on very low heat for approx. four or five minutes. Then turn off heat for zarda to achieve Dum as the heat dies out.

RICE WITH MILK
Kheer

I litre whole milk, homogenized
I litre half and half (milk and cream)
¾ cup rice, half broken in food processor
I cup sugar or as per taste
I tsp. butter
2 cardamoms, small seeded
I tbsp. kewra (screw pine essence)
10 pistachios, finely cut

Lightly fry cardamom seeds in butter on low heat and then on medium heat add the milk, half and half and the rice and let cooking take place, stirring from time to time preventing boiling over. As the milk and rice get thoroughly mixed forming a thick liquid, add sugar and mix well and let cooking continue on medium-low heat as the contents are somewhat halfway to a solid state. Add kewra and turn off heat. The kheer now made can be transferred into a bowl and sprinkled over with finely cut pistachios. The kheer should be kept in the refrigerator and the amount cooked according to the recipe will normally remain fit for eating up to ten days.

SEMOLINA HALWA
Sooji ka halwa

I cup semolina (sooji)
I cup sugar
I bar butter
4 tbsp. sliced almonds
I tsp. saffron
I tbsp. kewra (screw pine essence)
¼ cup raisins
2 cardamoms, small, seeded

Mix sugar in four cups of water and bring to boil on low heat. Add butter, cardamom seeds and saffron. In another pot brown semolina on low heat and then add to it the prepared water mixture and let cooking take place until the oil is separated. The halwa is then ready and it should preferably be spread while still warm on a cookie sheet and put into the refrigerator. When it cools and hardens it can be cut into desired pieces preferably in lozenge shape and may be kept in a freezer for long term use.

CARROT PUDDING
Gajar ka Halwa

5 lb. carrots, peeled and finely grated
l litre whole milk
¼ lb. butter
½ cup sugar
½ cup sliced almonds
½ cup green pistachios, whole

Put in together in a pot the grated carrots, milk and butter and let cooking of these three ingredients take place on medium heat, stirring from time to time until the moisture has evaporated and carrots have taken a greasy dry look. Now add sugar and mix it well and let cooking proceed to allow sugar to be fully absorbed in the carrots and all moisture has evaporated. This should be tested by putting a spoon through the cooked carrots and seeing it coming out clean with just the butter shining on the spoon. Add the almonds and pistachios and mix them well. Turn off heat leaving the pot on the burner until the heat dies out.

The carrot halwa can be frozen in the desired quantities in zippered bags and can be eaten as desired up to 5 months.

ISBN 142516918-X

9 781425 169183